LOCOMOTION PAPERS

NORTHERN NORTHUMBERLAND'S MINOR RAILWAYS:

Volume Two
Colliery & Associated Lines

by
Roger Jermy

THE OAKWOOD PRESS

© Oakwood Press & Roger Jermy 2011

British Library Cataloguing in Publication Data
A Record for this book is available from the British Library
ISBN 978 0 85361 704 4

Typeset by Oakwood Graphics.
Repro by PKmediaworks, Cranborne, Dorset.
Printed by Information Press Ltd, Eynsham, Oxford.

This book is dedicated to Toby, my third grandson.

From the same author
Northern Northumberland's Minor Railways:
  Volume One: Brickworks, Forestry, Contractors, Military Target railways and various other lines (ISBN 978 0 85361 703 7)

In preparation:
Northern Northumberland's Minor Railways:
  Volume Three: Sandstone, Whinstone and Gravel Lines

Northern Northumberland's Minor Railways:
  Volume Four: Limestone Industry Lines

Front cover: Hudswell, Clarke 0-6-0 side tank locomotive (Works No. 1823 of 1949), carrying number 38, simmers outside Shilbottle engine shed. Prior to its arrival at Shilbottle in 1971 it had worked at Wallsend, Burradon and Blyth. It left Shilbottle for preservation at Marley Hill, Tanfield Railway, in October 1973.   *David Tyreman*

Rear cover, top: One of Shilbottle Colliery's 'Austerity' locomotives, No. 46 (HE 2878/1943), is seen with a short train of 'vintage' tipper wagons. These internal-user wagons were used to transport colliery waste from the pithead to the spoil tip. In 1968 this locomotive was fitted with a Giesl ejector to improve steaming. The photograph was taken from the landsale staith close to where the line from Shilbottle to Southside crossed the Warkworth to Shilbottle road on the level. An information board is now located adjacent to the crossing.   *David Burdon Collection*

Rear cover, bottom: Ox-eye daisies decorate the ballast and bank sides as NCB locomotive No. 31 (RSH 7609/1950) pauses on the 'running road' at Whittle Colliery. On the left-hand side in the landsale siding is a rake of 21 ton hoppers, some being NCB- and some British Rail-owned. Next to the locomotive is the 'wagon storage road' and then the headshunt used before 'empties' were run down to the screens by gravity.   *Gordon Hall*

Published by The Oakwood Press (Usk), P.O. Box 13, Usk, Mon., NP15 1YS.
E-mail: sales@oakwoodpress.co.uk
Website: www.oakwoodpress.co.uk

Contents

Northern Northumberland
showing
Berwick and Alnwick Districts

Introduction

For the purpose of this book 'Northern Northumberland' is regarded as encompassing that area of the county lying within the administrative districts of Berwick-upon-Tweed and Alnwick. Until the mid-19th century part of the area covered lay within the County of Durham.

The term 'Minor Railways' is used here to include lines variously referred to as railways, tramways, wagonways and craneways, whether of narrow or standard gauge, which were not owned or operated by the 'main line' railway companies. Thus lines, such as the Rothbury branch, or Alnwick to Coldstream branch, do not feature as they were part of the North British Railway (NBR) and North Eastern Railway (NER) respectively. Later both became part of the London & North Eastern Railway (LNER) and British Railways (BR). A decision was made not to include the North Sunderland Railway (NSR) as its history has been fully described elsewhere (*see the Bibliography*). This line, though privately owned, was essentially a branch from a main line and was, for a time, operated by locomotives hired from the LNER. Similarly this book does not cover lines which were essentially worked as sidings from main lines, such as those servicing Easington Quarry at Belford, or the dockside branch railway at Tweedmouth. Finally the decision was taken not to include a treatment of underground railways or railways that predominantly ran underground, for example that at Elsdon Colliery.

Nevertheless a few liberties have been taken. For example the railway linking the Blaxter Quarry in Redesdale with Knowesgate station will be included even though, soon after leaving the quarry, it departs from the Alnwick District. Similarly the first volume included a description of both of the target railways on the Otterburn Training Ranges in Redesdale, even though one of them is located a few hundred metres outside the Alnwick District boundary. However, its inclusion is justified as this railway was first built and operated at Ross Links, on the North Northumberland coast south of Berwick, before being removed to Redesdale.

No attempt has been made to convert former imperial units into the present-day metric form. Units appropriate to the time of each railway have been used. Thus boiler pressures, for example, are referred to in pounds per square inch and costs are described in pounds, shillings and pence where the original source materials used these. Where metric units have appeared in original documents (such as the recent Heatherslaw Light Railway brochure which refers to the line as being 6.4 km in length) they have been retained.

The lines covered in these books were constructed for a wide variety of purposes. Some were associated with the many quarries, whether limestone, whinstone or sandstone, in the area. Others were linked with the coal mining industry. Some served brick and tile works, whilst others were built for military purposes. The forestry and timber industries were responsible for the creation of some lines and in recent years small lines have been constructed for the tourist industry. Almost exactly 200 years of local railway history are covered in these books.

Whilst it has been necessary to include some technical railway details it has also been considered important to place the railways into their social, geographical and historical context. Hopefully this will widen the readership of the book. The purist may consider it an important omission that lists of source materials and references have not been included after each chapter. If readers wish to make an individual study of the sources that have been consulted then they are cordially invited to get in touch with me via the publisher. Whilst researching for the books it has been considered a top priority that original sources be consulted, and that visits be made to as many of the sites as is practicable or possible. Oral ('anecdotal') evidence, and evidence from secondary sources, such as newspaper reports, has been used on various occasions. However, memories, particularly of events that happened nearly a century ago, may have become clouded, and every effort has been made to find written material which corroborates the evidence of the spoken word. On occasions it has been realised that the details reproduced here differ from previously published material. Hopefully, I am correcting earlier errors rather than introducing new ones; nevertheless I accept full responsibility for any mistakes in the text.

At many points in the books I have referred to lines or their remains being on private property. Permission must *always* be sought from landowners or tenants before visits are attempted. In certain cases the sites of railways, or former railways, can pose considerable danger to visitors, for example from steep cliffs, falling rocks, marshy ground or deep water. The surviving military railways pose a particular threat as they are located within still-active training areas where live ammunition is used. Visits to these lines are extremely dangerous if not carefully supervised by appropriate expert personnel. The flying of red flags, the display of red lights and the presence of secure fences indicate danger and the instructions on warning notices should be followed.

These books, whilst attempting to be comprehensive, cannot claim to have included every detail about these railways. Written records of some railways are sparse or incomplete, and, in the case of many of the lines, there is no one still alive with personal memories to impart. The author would therefore welcome the receipt of any information, perhaps from family histories or albums, which adds to the story of any of the lines. Old photographs or postcards, for which the author has been searching for several years, can provide valuable insight into the working of a line. Some, including those in Archives, Record Office and private collections, have proved impossible to reproduce satisfactorily. However, it would be a pleasure to receive details of any others that have survived.

In various places in the text, locomotive builders names have been abbreviated: a key to these abbreviations appears on page 126.

Roger Jermy
Alnwick, Northumberland
2010

Chapter One

The Coal Industry in
Northern Northumberland

For centuries, until the 1960s, the economy of the county of Northumberland was dependent on coal. The majority of the coal came from the south-east of the county, particularly from the area around the coal port of Blyth, with large pits being found at Ashington, Bedlington, Choppington, Ellington, Netherton and Pegswood. Other Northumberland pits were found in the Tyne valley, and near Berwick and Alnwick, these last two districts being covered by this volume.

Some coal, known as 'sea coal', has been collected on the Northumberland beaches for many years, largely for household use. Local coal measures outcropped beneath the sea and their erosion resulted in small pieces of coal being washed up by the tides. From early times small bell pits existed, such as those on Alnwick Moor, Shilbottle and Charlton Moor (to the north of Alnwick). These tapped coal seams near to the surface of the ground and the coal was raised using horse-powered winches or gins. Where coal seams outcropped to the surface drift mines were often created to follow the seam into the hillside to harvest the coal. Later deep shafts were excavated to obtain coal on a huge commercial scale. The last of these, located at Ellington, just to the south of the Alnwick district, closed on 26th January, 2005. The development of more complex collieries required, for example, the creation of systems for ventilating and draining the pits as well as the use of engines for raising coal to the surface. The increasingly extensive nature of the collieries required the employment of both underground and surface railway systems for moving the coal and miners, together with the necessary machinery for screening, washing and loading the coal onto rail or road vehicles. More recently, sites have developed for the exploitation of coal by the 'open cast' method.

Coal from the local area has found a variety of uses. Much was used locally for domestic heating and many collieries had a 'landsale yard'. In earlier years some use of coal was associated with the limeburning industry, which was well developed at various locations, especially near to the north Northumberland coast. Much local coal was exported from ports such as Tweedmouth and Amble, its destination being ports on the mainland of Europe as well as those in the south of England. Other coal was taken by rail to power stations, such as at Blyth or Stella, near Gateshead, for the generation of electricity. This tradition continues today in Northumberland with coal from huge open cast pits being transported to power stations, though no open cast pits are currently located in the Berwick and Alnwick Districts. Other coal was used to make coal gas.

Coal seams lie beneath much of the north of Northumberland. Several collieries were worked on a commercial scale to the south and south-west of Berwick. Further south, small collieries were associated with the lime industry at Seahouses, Beadnell and in the area of Ancroft. Numerous collieries developed in the Alnwick area, near to Shilbottle. Others were found close to Amble at Radcliffe, Broomhill and Hauxley. Finally several collieries were located in a line from Longframlington towards Elsdon including those at

Healeycote, Forestburngate and Longwitton. Many of these collieries were sufficiently large to warrant the use of waggonways or railways, both underground or on the surface. In early years men or horses were the source of motive power for the coal wagons. In later years some of the bigger collieries became linked with the national rail system and were busy enough to employ their own locomotives.

Some mines, though constructed mainly for the extraction of coal, produced other commercially important products. Those at Scremerston and Radcliffe, for example, yielded clay which allowed the creation of substantial brick and tile works close to the collieries. A nearby pit produced good quality ironstone as well as supplying coal for the Brinkburn Ironworks. The colliery railway or tramway systems were often employed for transporting these 'secondary products', such as the wagonway and later railway which transported clay from the Radcliffe Colliery to Amble Brickworks. Occasionally the use of colliery lines became shared, for example stone from the Forestburngate Quarry, was moved along the line of the Forestburngate Colliery Company.

HARBOUR, AMBLE "W" Amble Series

The coal staiths at Amble provide a grandstand view of a special event for the local young men wearing their 'Sunday-best'! A party of well-dressed visitors appears to be inspecting or joining some locally-registered fishing vessels. The men are in suits and some are wearing boaters. The ladies are wearing the long dresses of the period. The costume and the presence of both steam- and sail-powered vessels would suggest a date soon after 1900.   *Author's Collection*

Chapter Two

The Early Colliery Railways
of the Alnwick District

1 – The first Shilbottle to Alnwick Waggonway

The first records of coal mining in the Alnwick area appear to date from the mid-16th century. Prior to 1576 it is recorded that the Burgesses were working small pits on Alnwick Moor to the west of the town. The remains of bell pits, visible in the field known as 'Pitfall Field' to the north of the road linking the Great North Road with Shilbottle, may date from the same period. These are particularly visible in the low light of a setting sun. The Percy Estate records indicate that in 1567 a certain William Gray, of Alnwick, was working a coal mine at Shilbottle, said to be '...much profitable for the tenants there and for the inhabitants of the towns thereabouts.' However Shilbottle itself was described as '... a very poor towne ...' A 1585 survey referred to Shilbottle as having '...a very good and rich myne of coals, very profitable to the country thereabouts...'

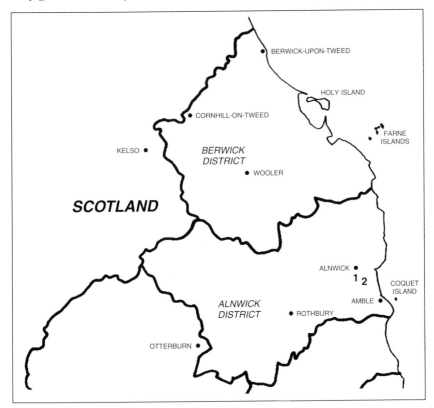

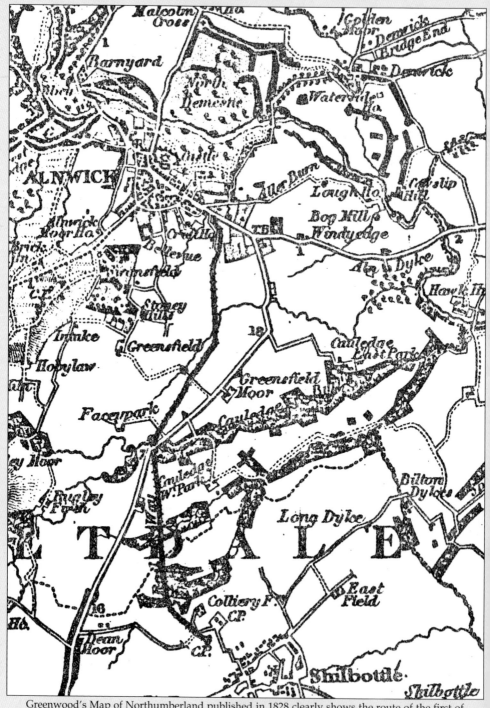

Greenwood's Map of Northumberland published in 1828 clearly shows the route of the first of the Shilbottle to Alnwick wagonways leading from the pit adjacent to Colliery Farm to its terminus on the southern fringe of Alnwick. *Northumberland Record Office*

By 1734 there were several small pits in the vicinity and there was an abundance of very good coals for local use. Much of the coal was taken into Alnwick in 'pokes' or sacks on the backs of asses or Galloways. Some of the coal was used in the local limekilns. In the poorer dwellings coal provided a source of both warmth and light. Prior to 1762 the main colliery was worked by the corporation; it is recorded that this provided much advantage to the town but little profit to the corporation! In 1762 the mines were transferred to the ownership of the Duke of Northumberland, who, in 1776, purchased some land and a small homestead known as 'Shilbottle Lodge' from Messrs C. Henry, Hugh and Thomas John Taylor, a family whose name will be mentioned again in the story of mining at Shilbottle. A certain William Brown also worked a colliery at Shilbottle known as 'Windmill Pit'; this was opened on 22nd June, 1763. It was located in a field to the west of Dean Moor near a well known as 'Taffy's Well'. It is recorded that Brown used a windmill to work the pump to draw water from the mine.

A document, in the Watson Engineering Collection dated 30th September, 1802, refers to the working expenses of Shilbottle Pit (known locally as 'Blue Lodge Pit'). It records that a total annual profit of £1,325 was expected. The colliery expenses included repairs and coals for a 'machine engine', a landsale man, Galloways and boys for 'putting' coal to the base of the shaft, and also the '…repairing and laying of waggonways'. These were presumably underground or internal to the colliery site. The 'machine engine' may well have referred to the early Newcomen Engine known to have been used at Shilbottle. At least six shafts were said to be located nearby.

In the same year, 1802, local newspapers carried an advert for a 'VALUABLE LANDSALE COLLIERY' to be leased for a term of 21 years from Michaelmas 1802:

> That extensive current-going colliery called Shilbottle Colliery. This colliery from the acknowledged superiority of the coal and its local situation (lying contiguous to the Market Town of Alnwick) commands a very extensive and valuable trade which is likely to increase. The tenant will be accommodated with a sufficient quantity of land for carrying on of the colliery. For particulars apply to Thomas Taylor of Newburn, near Newcastle. And proposals in writing must be sent to His Grace the Duke of Northumberland, Northumberland House, London, on or before 20th August next. The Lease will be restrained from increasing the present price of coals or from assigning over the Colliery or engaging partners without a licence under His Grace's hand for that purpose.
> *Newburn. 31 May 1802.*

The lease was taken up by John Taylor.

It is perhaps useful to explain at this point that many of the pits and mines in the vicinity were, at some time, known as 'Shilbottle Colliery'. In 1807 the pit at Shilbottle to be served by the first Alnwick waggonway was sunk; this (at NU189089) was alternatively known as 'Engine Pit' or 'Blue Lodge Pit'. Later a new shaft appears to have been sunk very close by, referred to as 'Smoke Staple Pit' which may have been a ventilation shaft. In 1844 'Tate's Pit' (otherwise known as 'Shilbottle Townhead Pit' or simply 'Town Pit') was sunk at NU194083. A year later at NU198096 East Pit (also known as 'Engine Pit' or 'New Engine Pit') was sunk. 'Long Dyke Pit' at NU207101 (at different times

The stable block, built adjacent to Colliery Farm to house the horses employed on the first Shilbottle waggonway, still survives some 200 years after its construction. Although in a good state of repair, currently it appears to be disused.   *Author*

referred to as 'Longdyke Pit', 'Longdike Pit' or even 'Bilton Banks') was sunk in August 1844; this was the source of the coal transported by the second Alnwick waggonway. After the closure of Long Dyke the name of 'Shilbottle Colliery' was applied to the newer 'Grange Pit'.

It was in July 1809, just two years after the commencement of a new shaft at Shilbottle, that the Newcastle newspapers reported the opening of the first Alnwick waggonway or 'railroad':

On Monday 5th May the inhabitants of Alnwick and its vicinity were gratified by completion of an undertaking hitherto not attempted in the north, viz. the delivery of coals at Alnwick from Shilbottle Colliery by wagons conveyed along a metal railroad. The immense sums annually paid for this indispensable necessity of life in the county town of Northumberland have long been severely felt and of later years have produced the effect of almost depriving the poorer classes of the community of so essential a comfort in this chill climate: coals have lately been sold to a consumer at the exhorbitant [*sic*] rate of 2 guineas a Newcastle chaldron (a price unexampled in any other part of the county) nearly one half of which was charged by hired cartmen for leading. The railroad passes invariably through the grounds of His Grace, Duke of Northumberland, the proprietor of the mine; and by its judicious directions, the distance is only three miles from the colliery to the staith, possessing the most important advantage that not a shilling of wayleave is paid. Coals have already considerably fallen in price; and the whole of this spirited and laudable undertaking has been planned and executed by, and at the sole expense of, Mr. John Taylor, the lessee of Shilbottle Colliery.

John Taylor is known to have worked the Shilbottle Colliery for only about eight years as an advertisement appeared in the Newcastle newspapers in 1815:

LANDSALE COLLIERY

To be let for a term of 21 years and entered upon January 1st 1817.

The old established current-going Colliery of Shilbottle in the County of Northumberland with a farm containing 240 acres appended.

The mine is most excellent quality and the vend very considerable, the colliery being distant only 3 miles from Alnwick and connected therewith by means of a Cast Iron Waggon Way [sic].

The colliery may be viewed and a Plan of the Working seen by applying to the Overman upon the premises and Mr Tate of Bank House will show the Lands.

The particulars of letting may be known by a Reference to Messrs Smith and Laws, Alnwick Castle, who will receive proposals for the Colliery and Land respectively until the 1st February 1816.

Alnwick Castle 13th November 1815.

A later advertisement, dated 2nd March, 1816, amended the farm size to 100 acres and altered the date for receipt of proposals from 1st February to 1st August.

The lease appears to have been taken up by Thomas and Hugh Taylor for a receipt exists, dated 18th March, 1818, for Shilbottle coals: 16 cwt at 4½d., total 6s. which is signed over their name. The *Parson & White Trade Directory* for 1827 included '...the excellent colliery here is held by His Grace under a lease by Messrs T. & H. Taylor, who employ about 70 of the inhabitants. The principle [sic] coal seam is 32" thick and is of good quality'.

The waggonway, or railroad as it is often called, appears on Greenwoods Map of Northumberland published in 1828 and on the tithe map of 1844. Details of the location of the staith and 'railroad' near to Alnwick appear on John Woods Map of Alnwick dated 1827 and on the 1849 'Cholera Plan' (based on Woods Map). Although the line had been closed and lifted by the time of the publication of the 1st Edition of the Ordnance Survey (OS), much of its route can be followed on these maps.

In 2008 a local historian walking along the alignment of the first Shilbottle wagonway discovered some rusty metal poking up from the ground. On closer examination it has turned out to be short fragments of plates from the cast-iron plateway.   *Author*

Above: The site of the staith, located at the northern end of Wagonway Road, was used successively by the colliery wagonway and then the North Eastern Railway, LNER and British Railways. In this photograph, dating from the BR era, three coal hoppers are positioned over the coal drops.

John Mallon, courtesy of Vera Mallon

Right: The former coal office at Wagonway Road later became the weigh office for the adjacent weighbridge. This undated picture shows some of the staff posed in front of the office. The building's chimney partly hides the end of the staith.

John Mallon Collection, courtesy of Vera Mallon

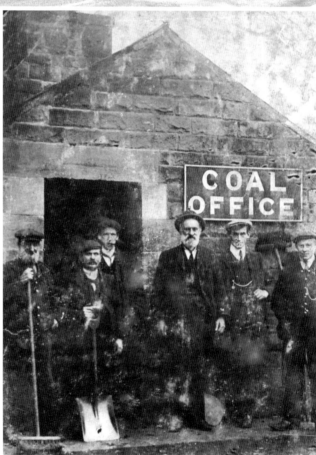

From the colliery at Shilbottle the line headed north-westwards, passing Colliery Farm, then north, passing to the east of the house known as West Cawledge Park adjacent to the Great North Road. It crossed this road close to the Cawledge bridge and continued in a north-easterly direction following the easiest alignment, then continued on due north. It passed through fields known as Stanley Flats, Midding Stead and Mosey Land, following the alignment of the eastern side of the present-day Wagonway Road, to a staith some 300 yards south of Alnwick's Hotspur Tower. Wagonway Road itself originated as an old field lane. The gradient was in favour of the loaded wagons as far as Cawledge. The land then rose gently before a largely level section to the staith. One secondary source states that the horse-drawn wooden waggons could hold up to 60 cwt of coal and that they had hand brakes, operated by a boy who walked alongside the wagons. The same source, however, claims that the rails were wooden, yet sources contemporary to the line all refer to metal, or more specifically cast-iron, rails. In 2008 a local historian, whilst walking along the route of the former trackbed, discovered some pieces of well-rusted cast iron, bound together by clay. It is quite likely that these are fragments of the originals rails which have lain, undiscovered, for many years. Photographs have been sent to the historical experts at the National Railway Museum and confirmation of the identity of the rails is awaited. They appear to identify the line as a plateway, in which the waggons, with unflanged wheels, were kept on the track by means of a flange on the side of the rails. The gauge of the line is not known. No sleepers have yet been discovered.

The colliery continued to be successful. The rent, payable to 'His Grace' was £210 per annum with an additional sum of 4½d. per ton of coal raised. There was no wayleave rent for carrying the coal on the waggonway across the Duke's land to Alnwick staith.

On 24th July, 1838 a newspaper advertisement read: 'Coal Workmen: A few steady hewers and putters who can work a 30" seam, will meet with good encouragement by applying at Shilbottle Colliery'.

By 1842 several cottages had been constructed for the workmen close to the colliery. Around that time a banksman could earn 4s. per day with a rolleyman underground earning 3s. 4d. In both cases this was for a shift of 12 hours.

A letter, appeared in the *Gateshead Observer* newspaper in 1846, addressed to the Editor:

Sir,
    Although coal abounds in the neighbourhood of Alnwick, yet, from restrictions, the inhabitants have long been obliged to bring their principle [sic] supply from Shilbottle, a pit belonging to His Grace, the Duke of Northumberland, a distance of four miles and a half by the Turnpike Road – or by a railway of 3 miles - for which the following charges are made:

    At the pit mouth 7/6d per ton. If conveyed by the railroad to the staith an addition of 2/6d per ton with 1/- for delivery in the town, making altogether 11/-.

    Perhaps some of your readers will reply to this letter and state the price of coal with a similar length of railroad, or whether it would be possible, on the opening of the Newcastle and Berwick Railway that coal could be brought from Newcastle at a more moderate price than what is now charged here. The distance by the main trunk is about 30 miles to Bilton station and the branch then to Alnwick three miles.
    I am, Sir, your obedient servant.
    XYZ [sic],   Alnwick, 23rd December 1846.

This letter perhaps indicates why the demise and final closure of the waggonway was not far away. The Bilton Junction (later Alnmouth) to Alnwick branch railway (then under construction) was clearly a potential competitor. The precise date of closure of the waggonway seems not to have been recorded though it certainly took place in the late 1840s or early 1850s. A Mines Report dated 1851 referred to Shilbottle having a small landsale colliery with two shafts, but made no reference to the waggonway. The site of the staith at Alnwick was later used for the North Eastern Railway's own staith where coals, brought along the branch to Alnwick, could be discharged. This staith was linked by a siding to other lines of rails in the small station yard. This staith, with a small nearby office, survived into LNER and then BR days.

The *Alnwick Journal* of 15th March, 1860 (and also several later editions) contained a series of articles under the heading 'Something about Shilbottle', the first being a chapter being entitled 'Down the Pit'. These articles referred to journeys made from Alnwick to the Shilbottle Colliery and contained some useful information. For example the first article referred to,

> …fields which once upon a time had the 'waggonway' through them, to convey the coals to a staith at Bond gate End, from whence it was carried through the town in cuddy carts by superannuated originals, who retailed it in miniature 'pokes' containing, they said, five halfpence worth… The race is now extinct or nearly so – (just) one carrying on the business...

A second reference was to a muddy cart road known as 'the coal road' which perhaps refers to landsale coal leaving the colliery by road. It went on to refer to the 'rollaway' with iron rails inside the pit and the small trucks propelled along them by the 'putters'. The labour force at the colliery was 44 hewers, 31 putters, six trapper lads, and 26 'offhands' (including the banksmen, engineman, drivers and others). Nearby the houses for the men were provided rent-free with free coals and use of a small garden. The author described the pitmen's homes as '…generally very comfortable, well stocked with valuable furniture…' The largest house was the residence of the Manager, Mr W. Wilson. However the pit referred to is almost certain to be the new Long Dyke pit, one of the several shafts sunk by the Taylors in the 1840s, for the second chapter refers to the author walking along the waggonway to '… where the old pit was worked, and where, for many years, almost all the coal used in Alnwick was brought to bank'.

Traces of the waggonway must have survived until the 1880s for a newspaper report of an 1886 journey over the newly opened Alnwick to Cornhill railway referred to the line '…passing over the old waggonway'. In addition a brief reference was made to the line in the *Alnwick Gazette* of 31st March, 1888. This states that the waggonway was not used and that neither the ratepayers, nor the North Eastern Railway nor the freeholders own it. However, in July 1896 Alnwick is recorded as having a public house called 'The Waggonway'.

Today, with the aid of maps, it is possible to follow some of the route of the old waggonway, though it crosses private land (including sports grounds and farmland) for much of its length and the necessary permissions to visit must be obtained. Wagonway Road [*sic*], constructed after the demise of the line, follows

The street sign, 'Wagonway Road', is mounted on a wall directly opposite the northern terminus of the first Shilbottle to Alnwick wagonway. The staith has long since disappeared, being replaced by a small car park.   *Author*

the alignment of the most northerly part of the route. The site of the old staith at the end of this road is now a small parking area, used principally by visitors to Barter Books, the second-hand bookshop. The present-day Colliery Farm lies adjacent to the former pit site. Some of the site remains can be identified. The former colliery office is now part of a boarding cattery, and the former brick-built stable building for the horses used on the waggonway still survives adjacent to the farm approach road. One shaft remained open here until it was capped in about 1935. Parts of various former spoil tips exist.

2 – *The second Alnwick to Shilbottle Waggonway*

In the mid-1860s one of the Taylor family was still the lessee of the Long Dyke colliery at Shilbottle. The family was described in the 1864 *Slater's Directory* as 'Coal Owners'. Elsewhere they were referred to as 'Coal viewers to the Duke of Northumberland'. By this time they were expanding their coal interests to include Warkworth and Amble. Hugh lived in the road known as Bondgate Within, then moved to Bailiffgate, in Alnwick, whilst Thomas' address was stated as Shilbottle Colliery. Their agent at Shilbottle was William Wilson. Hugh had died by 1866 leaving his brother to carry on the business.

In 1867 the colliery area at Shilbottle covered 2,221 acres underground, with 921 acres of coal having been raised, amounting to 3.5 million tons. The reserves were estimated as another 5 million tons. In 1864 the overall cost of producing the coal was 4s. 7d. per ton, but by 1868 it had risen to 7s. 1d. per ton because of water inflow and increased haulage costs as a result of steeper gradients underground. The selling prices were 8s. 4d. per ton for best coals and 3s. 4d. for small coals (which represented just 4 per cent of the total). The mean was 8s. 2d. per ton so that, in 1868, the profit was 1s. 1d. per ton. The current value of the plant at the colliery was £4,776 16s. 2d. It was over half a mile from the shaft to the working faces.

Underground there was a railway system of 3 ft 8 in. gauge (is this a clue as to the gauge of the first waggonway?) with 2,800 yards of 22 lb. rail. There were 24 rolleys (underground 'carriages' for the transport of coal-filled 'corves' which were hazel baskets), 40 'trams' (with wooden sides) and 36 'tubs'. Eight pit horses worked underground with a further two being employed on the surface. The

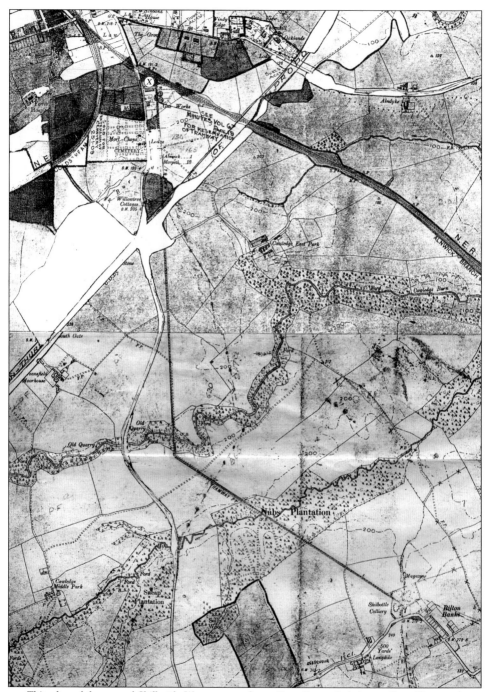

This plan of the second Shilbottle Waggonway shows its entire route between the colliery and the depot site (*X*) adjacent to both the Alnwick gas works and the NER branch railway. Note that Bilton Banks village, near to the colliery, appears to be only partially completed.

D.P. Dalby Collection

amount of coal raised per annum in the mid-1860s was approximately 20,000 tons. There were several seams but only one, the 'Shilbottle Seam' was of commercial value. It was 2 ft 5 in. thick in 1868 and was at a depth of about 25 fathoms (150 ft). The colliery had several open shafts. The 'coal shaft' at Long Dyke was 10½ ft in diameter and had a 40 hp engine to raise the coal. There was an engine shaft of 7½ ft diameter with a beam engine and two sets of water pumps. There was also a ventilation shaft in Shilbottle village which was 5½ ft in diameter with a furnace at the top for creating an up-draught to remove stale air from the pit.

The question of connecting Shilbottle Colliery at Long Dyke with the North Eastern Railway system by means of a branch was considered. However, it was dismissed on the grounds that the benefit to be derived from an extended trade would not be commensurate with the additional capital expenditure required. A railway, crossing the Duke's land, was estimated to cost about £7,000 and would involve a descent of 300 ft involving substantial gradients.

However, a line of railway was constructed by the 1870s linking the colliery, not with the rails of the NER, but with a Landsale depot on the south side of Alnwick. By this time the Shilbottle Coal Company, had been formed by Messrs Henry Augustus Paynter, a solicitor living at 'Freelands', Alnwick, and Nathaniel Dunn, a retired solicitor living at Netherton House, Bedlington. Later the company also involved a certain Ellen Garwood from London. This concern took over the operation of the colliery at Long Dyke from the Taylors. The precise date of opening of the rail line appears not to have been recorded but in the 1870s the records of the Alnwick Gas Company make references to the line being operational. This company had operated from premises in Alnwick from about 1820, being located at the corner of Ratten Row and Canongate opposite St Michael's Church. Its coal (sourced from Killingworth or Whitwell) was carted to the works from Alnmouth. However, in 1870 it wished to relocate to be near to the NER which operated the branch from Bilton Junction to Alnwick. The company enquired from the railway the cost of laying a siding for coal delivery to a site close to the South Turnpike leading from Alnwick. (There was no question of it using Shilbottle coal as it was not suited to the purpose.) In 1878 the gas company looked at a field of two acres which was occupied by a certain William Links. This field adjoined the main south turnpike and lay close to the NER branch. William Ford, a gas engineer of Stockton, inspected the site, also the adjacent town manure depot and the depot of the Shilbottle Coal Company. Subsequent meetings took place between the Secretary of the gas company, the representative of the estate office of the Duke of Northumberland (who initially opposed the use of the site), the NER and the Shilbottle Coal Company. The coal company was asked to move its waggonway (often referred to as the 'tramway'), its approach road (using a field of Mr Luke), coal staith and drop. The company declined to do this. (The foregoing indicates that the line was certainly in place and operating by 1878.)

On 24th April, 1879 the gas company applied to construct its new works on the South Turnpike site, all to be completed at the company's expense. The works, with a retort, buildings, circular storage tanks and sidings from the NER, was built after permission was granted. The coal company was agreeable that the works could be constructed at the sides of its line with easy passage for the coal-carrying trucks from 'Longdike' [sic]. A map of 1882 shows the Shilbottle

On 1st July, 1923 a photographer attempted to take a picture of some cable-hauled wagons on the waggonway crossing over the bridge across one of the branches of the Cawledge Burn; this was the result. Although of poor quality it is the only picture that the author has been able to trace of the waggonway 'in action'. A footbridge over the burn is in the foreground.

D.P. Dalby Collection

This view of Long Dyke Colliery at Shilbottle was taken just before closure in the mid-1920s. This would appear to show the landsale part of the colliery sidings with a horse-drawn cart awaiting its load. Various tubs are in view with the lines for the wagonway towards Alnwick disappearing to the right.

Richard Hay Collection

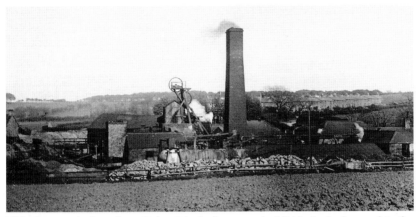

This photograph shows Long Dyke pit in the foreground whilst in the background, to the right, are the new-looking houses of Bilton Banks village which were built to house the colliery employees. Apart from the Colliery Manager's house all has since disappeared from the landscape. *Author's Collection*

company's line passing between the storage tanks and other buildings of the gas company to sidings at the coal depot. The coal depot maintained its exit onto the turnpike road. The bridge, conveying the gas company's siding over the waggonway, was constructed in 1881.

In 1882 the pit was managed by William A. Ritson. By 1888 John Roscamp was Manager and he held the same position in 1896 when the pit employed 95 men working below ground and 41 on the surface. By 1902 William Dixon was Manager and the respective figures were 116 and 39. At the start of World War I Dixon was still Manager but the numbers employed had reached 216 underground and 88 on the surface.

To return to the 1870s: at the other end of the waggonway line, at Shilbottle, the coal mine was having other effects. An 1874 report by sanitary inspector Frederick Richard Wilson contained the following: 'The present prosperity of the pit has caused a demand for houses and too much crowding for want of them.' He went on to say that he had seen '…dwellings of a very insanitary kind…(and)…a rotten old privy, choked drains, manure heaps and water in a well not fit for drinking…'. This description contrasts with the rosier picture painted some 30 years before this! The drinking water supply for the village came from three 'pants' (fountains) described as in 'fair' condition. To alleviate the housing shortage a new village, Bilton Banks, was constructed close to the Longdike Pit. This consisted of two parallel rows of terraced dwellings, 17 in 'Long Row', six in 'Short Row', with a larger house for the colliery Manager.

This second railway, also variously referred to as either a tramway or waggonway, was built as a double-track line with a gauge of 2 ft. Cable haulage was always employed. Ash was used for ballast. It left Longdike pit (by now often referred to colloquially as 'Bilton Banks Pit') and ran in a north-westerly direction towards and through Nubs Plantation where a burn in the steep-sided valley was bridged. From an initial height of 220 ft it reached the 200 ft contour at the plantation. From here it crossed a couple of fields before turning to follow an almost direct northerly course. Almost immediately it crossed a second burn in a steep wooded valley on a high wooden bridge. These two valleys are

Headed notepaper of the Shilbottle Coal Company.   *Northumberland Record Office*

known locally as 'The Callishes', (a corruption of 'Cawledge'; the burns are referred to as the first and second Cawledge Burns). The approaches to the bridges involved short inclines. Having emerged from the trees the line continued northwards crossing several fields. There was a couple of short tunnels where small roads passed over the line, close to Cawledge East Park Road, before arriving at the coal depot (close to the 200 ft contour).

It is fortunate that the memories of several of the former employees have been preserved. Mr W.H. Dixon recalled that at the colliery there were two Greenwood & Batley turbines which generated electricity. Electric motors drove the 5 ft diameter drum around which was looped the 1 inch diameter steel cable or 'endless rope'. This endless rope, running on pulleys, extended to the coal depot where there was a second drum. Each truck, which each held four to five hundredweights of coal, was attached onto this 'rope' with a 'snatch clamp' (often referred to as a 'hambone' because of its shape) which needed to be secured tightly. Mr Tennant recalls this clamp being centrally mounted on a raised bracket and fitted with a locking lever. At the front and rear of each truck were 'rope guides'. Occasionally the trucks would break loose, 'run wild' and crash into each other. Men were stationed at each of the inclines to check that the clamps had not worked loose; they tended to hammer the locking lever whether the clamp was loose or not! No-one was ever injured as a result of this but accidents occasionally caused delays. The rails were made of steel and the trucks ran over them in pairs, generally one with wooden sides and one with steel sides. The pairs generally ran about 30 to 40 yards apart. At the colliery the loaded trucks would be attached to the cable and hauled to the coal depot. Here the 'fulls' ran up a small incline where they were unhitched and forwarded into a 'tumbler cage' where the contents were discharged into hoppers, from which the coal was loaded into sacks. The empty trucks were then reattached to the cable and hauled back to the colliery where they were knocked loose. They ran down beneath a colliery hopper where they were filled prior to their next journey back to the depot. In later years communication between pit and depot was by means of a telephone and bell system. The cables were strung from oak poles obtained from nearby Swarland Woods.

There were many instances of pilfering from the trucks whilst in transit. Occasionally the thieves were caught and brought to justice. For example, the *Alnwick Gazette* reported on 17th March, 1917 that a certain John Patterson, a joiner of Union Court, Alnwick, was charged with stealing 4½ stone of coal (value 8*d*.) from the tramway; he was found guilty and fined 24*s*.

Others used the line to obtain 'free rides' though two men were forced to remain overnight in one of the close-fit tunnels when the cable and wagons stopped moving at the end of the day's shift, trapping them inside! Slight injuries were also caused when insufficient clearances at the side of wagons caused cuts and abrasions to persons unable to get out of the way.

The colliery Manager in the last days of the Shilbottle Colliery Company was Mr John Armstrong Dixon. He was finally replaced when the concern was taken over by the Cooperative Wholesale Society (CWS) in 1916. The clerk at the coal depot office in later years was a Mr Storey who lived at nearby Royal Oak Cottage. Also at the coal depot a 'depot weighman' was employed and details of his job specification have survived:

> To attend fully the Coal Company's business and its phases as attached to the Depot, in cart and railway, To regularly attend each working day on the starting of the Tramway. In winter weather to turn out at such times as necessary to secure the running of the Tramway when any stoppages occur or are likely to occur by snowstorms, breakdown etc.

One interesting sideline concerns a visit made by King Edward VII to Alnwick Castle when he was greatly impressed by the quality of Shilbottle coal being burned on the castle fires. He requested that a contract be drawn up for best Shilbottle coal to be supplied for the fireplaces at Buckingham Palace. This coal, specially graded, passed through the accounts of Alnmouth, formerly Bilton, station!

In 1913 the Shilbottle Coal Company (still owned by Ellen Garwood, Henry Augustus Paynter and Nathaniel Dunn) negotiated a new lease from the Duke of Northumberland. It was to include the lease of the mines at Shilbottle together with the surface lands and buildings including the colliery Manager's house and pit heap and other items. They would have permission to extract both coal and fireclay (but not lime), be allowed to deepen the existing pits and sink one or two new pits at Sturton Grange within the Shilbottle Parish. Their rights were maintained to,

> …use the present existing tramway…through…the wayleave lands…for the loading and carrying away of the produce of the mines, either to the town of Alnwick, or to a siding on the Alnwick branch of the North Eastern Railway now used by the Lessees. [They could also] …build such other tramway or railway as shall be necessary for loading and carrying away the produce of the new shafts to a siding on the main line of the North Eastern Railway….

They were also granted permission to build gutters, staithes, gins, steam engines and buildings. They would be limited to the extraction of 10,000 tons of coal per annum. There were also stipulations regarding the wagons having proper wheels, prohibiting the use of stationary engines or rope haulage where there were level crossings over roadways. The lease also allowed the lessor, i.e. the Duke's estate, to cross over the railways, tramways or roads at any time, providing the passage did not interfere with the engines or wagons of the Lessee. Finally the lessor should retain the powers to inspect the pit at any time.

It was in 1916 that the CWS negotiated to purchase the rights to Longdike for just £50 and shortly afterwards their Mr C.S. Anderson took over as colliery Manager. In the same year, the concern was told to reduce the quantity of coal for sale in the Northumberland area so that more coal could be diverted to the furnaces of the munitions factories. Shilbottle best coal had been selling for 22s. per ton at this time

Eleven of the staff of the Shilbottle Coal Co. pose for the photographer in front of two small coal tubs and the wall of the coal depot south of Alnwick. This depot was closed soon after the demise of Longdike Colliery and its waggonway.   *D.P. Dalby Collection*

The village of Bilton Banks was built to house the men at the nearby pit. After the closure of the pit all buildings were demolished apart from the former Manager's house which survives today in private ownership.   *Ken Middlemist Collection*

with nuts fetching 18s. per ton. However, by this time the writing was on the wall for Longdike, for extraction of the coal was becoming more difficult and the equipment was becoming out-of-date. In 1919 the shafts of a new Shilbottle Pit, called Grange Pit, were being sunk and between 1922 and 1924 coal production at Longdike Pit declined. In 1921 a total of 109 men were working in the pit, on the tramway and at Alnwick coal depot. Between November 1924 and February 1925 the men were switched from this pit to the new Grange Pit (NU214080), which was fully operational by 1926. Longdike Pit (by now referred to as 'The Old Pit') was closed on 31st August, 1925 and its equipment was dismantled. The waggonway closed at this time. Most of the rails were lifted and the bridges and short tunnels were demolished or fell down. In 1944 the question of the land, formerly traversed by the waggonway at the coal depot, was raised by the gas company. Mr Turnbull of this company met with Mr Beresford-Pierce of the Northumberland Estates Office to try and reach an agreement over the rights to the ground. This was done and on 6th June of that year signed copies of the agreement were exchanged to transfer the land to the gas company.

Although most of the Longdike coal had been sold locally in the town of Alnwick and in the neighbouring farms and villages, some coal had latterly been taken away from the coal depot by the NER. The Shilbottle Coal Company had had one, later two, short sidings constructed (in about 1901) from the Alnwick branch, adjacent to the gas company's sidings, one of which was subsequently extended.

Today all traces of the Longdike Colliery buildings have disappeared except for the Manager's house, now in private ownership. The colliery site has been planted with trees. The route of the waggonway can be followed across nearby fields into Cawledge Wood where a gate straddles the former trackbed. The route through the wood, involves steep slopes, copious vegetation (including newly planted alder and coniferous trees) and wet conditions underfoot. It is difficult to follow its course exactly on both sides of the burn, but its route can be traced more easily across the fields to the north, where it follows the present day field boundaries. The route through the second 'Callish' is somewhat easier with the footbridge providing a convenient crossing of the Cawledge Burn. It is in this area that, until recently, some relics survived in the form of poles with pulleys. At least one length of rail was present submerged in the burn. All traces of the bridges and their abutments have disappeared. The trackbed can be followed for a short distance as it climbs the gradient and leaves the Callish, though locked gates, blocking the public footpath, can make passage difficult. The route then follows the field boundary in the direction of the new trading estate and A1 Alnwick by-pass. Close to the site of the former coal depot it is possible to discern the route of the line as it passes between the several surviving buildings from the former gas works. Much of the route lies on land belonging to the Northumberland Estates and their tenant farmers. Other land belongs to British Gas, and the site of the coal depot, adjacent to the former Alnwick branch railway, belongs to Kitsons, manufacturers of double-glazing units and similar products. For most sections of the line permission must be sought to walk and inspect the former trackbed. Only short lengths are now designated as public footpaths and these are clearly signposted.

Fortunately a short length of rail has been preserved and is safe in private ownership.

Peckett 0-4-0 saddle tank *Olive* (P 1790/1935) was the third locomotive to be bought new by the Cooperative Wholesale Society for work at Shilbottle Colliery. It was one of the two CWS locomotives at Shilbottle at the time of nationalization. *Olive* is shown here when visiting Ashington for repairs in July 1950.   *Beamish Museum Collection*

Gwen was a product of Robert Stephenson & Hawthorns Ltd which replaced a former scrapped locomotive with the same name. It left Shilbottle in July 1952 for repairs. It is shown here at Ashington in April 1953 soon after these repairs had been completed. Like *Olive* it was eventually scrapped in 1964.   *Beamish Museum Collection*

Chapter Three

The 20th Century Colliery Railways
at Shilbottle (from 1915 onwards)

The story of the Shilbottle Collieries, from 1915 to the present day, starts with the ownership of the Longdike Pit by the Shilbottle Coal Co. of Garwood, Paynter and Dunn (*see Chapter One*). This out-of-date pit was closed and the new Shilbottle Colliery to the south-east of the village (NU214080) was opened. This new pit was sometimes called Grange Pit, or occasionally in documents, New Pit. It had two shafts shaft, 945 ft deep, and was in full production by 1926. A new company called South Shilbottle Collieries was formed, later reconstituted as South Shilbottle Collieries (1928) Ltd. It had opened the new drift at Whittle (NU175065), between Shilbottle and Newton-on-the-Moor, and also owned the Framlington Pit at Longframlington. It was put up for sale in 1928 and purchased by the Cooperative Wholesale Society. The sale proposal was reported in the *Alnwick Gazette* for 28th January, 1928, and the purchase recorded in the edition of the 15th December of the same year. However the CWS appear to have been operating the colliery before this date, perhaps under the terms of a lease or agreement. Framlington Pit, with its unusual overhead cableway (q.v.), was soon closed and the other two collieries, Shilbottle and Whittle, remained in CWS ownership until nationalization of the coal industry by the Labour Government after World War II.

Nationalization, and the formation of the National Coal Board (NCB), produced some investment and improvements, firstly at Shilbottle and then at Whittle, where a new drift was sunk in 1965 (NU174067). At its peak Shilbottle produced some 272,000 tons of coal per year and over 800 men worked there. Whittle's peak production reached about 700,000 tons per year with a maximum of nearly 650 being employed. In 1978 an underground connection was driven between these two pits and the mines were effectively merged; some 1,100 men now worked at the 'combined' pit though this was shortly reduced to 800. On 28th August, 1981 closure of Shilbottle was announced. Then on 4th October, 1982 Shilbottle ceased raising its own coal, all being brought out via Whittle. The closure of Whittle by British Coal (which had taken over from the NCB in 1986) was announced and coal production ceased almost immediately on 10th January, 1987. The colliery closed completely on 27th March after some salvage work had been performed. Since that time, the pit has been reopened and small quantities of high-quality coal have been produced by private companies, firstly ERS Mining Developments (NE) Ltd, then Whittle Colliery Ltd. The site is proposed for possible development as a leisure complex with hotels, fishing facilities and other amenities, though suggestions have also been made that coal production may restart.

The demise of Longdike and of Framlington Pit resulted in the closure of the second Alnwick waggonway and the overhead cableway respectively. Two new standard gauge mineral railways were constructed: the first, from Shilbottle Grange Pit to the East Coast main line being just less than two miles long, with the second, a more winding line from Whittle Drift to the same main line, being 4½ miles long. All of the collieries mentioned obtained their coal from the Shilbottle seam.

3 – The Shilbottle Colliery Railway

> The railway and other surface arrangements are well forward, everything being done on substantial lines with a view to permanency and reduction of future working costs.

This extract from a report on the new Shilbottle (Grange Pit) Colliery was dated 9th March, 1923, when the colliery and its railway line were still under

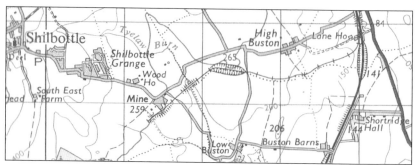

The NCB Shilbottle line.   *Ordnance Survey, Crown Copyright, all rights reserved*

construction. At this time production at the old pit at Longdike was being run down and many men had already transferred to the new pit. Sinking of its first shaft had begun in 1919 and work was well advanced on the second, adjacent shaft. Both shafts were to be fitted with winders, though one would be principally for ventilation purposes. By 1926 the switch over of men was complete, the new pit was in full production and the coal was being successfully taken out by rail.

Construction of the railway started at several locations and the 1921-22 edition of the OS maps provides an excellent 'snapshot' of the works in progress at several points along the line. The first rails were laid at the pit itself, forming several sidings and a small locoshed was built, ready for the arrival of the first locomotive in 1923. The alignment necessitated the building of a substantial embankment leading from the pit. Lengths of track were also being laid where the line was to cross the Tyelaw Burn. A level crossing was in the process of construction on the road south of Buston. Shortly afterwards the gaps were filled and the exchange point was constructed at Lane House Sidings (named after a local building), to the south of Alnmouth station. Sidings were later laid on the south side of the branch leading to the site of some colliery spoil tips.

Leaving the mine, the line almost immediately passed over a level crossing with the Warkworth to Shilbottle road. It headed in a north-easterly direction passing the first spoil tip on the right-hand side. (In the 1960s a loop was constructed at this point to facilitate locomotives running round spoil trains.) There was then a sharp change in direction as it swung around to head east-south-easterly passing the sidings of the second spoil tip immediately before the second level crossing over the road linking High and Low Buston. Then, passing to the south of High Buston its direction changed again to easterly, then north-easterly as it approached the main line and the Lane House interchange sidings (often referred to simply as 'New Lane').

Just before these sidings there was one arm of a loop (known as siding C - *see plan overleaf*) where empty wagons were placed by the main line engine. The full wagons were left by the main line engine in the other road (known as siding J). The colliery engine which had brought the 'fulls' would then return back to the colliery with the empties. The main line engine would enter the sidings via a facing crossover from the down main line. It would draw the empties forward into either of the sidings known as A and B which formed another loop. The shunt head beyond was known as siding H which extended almost as far north as the level crossing at Wooden. Empty wagons would then be propelled back into siding C. The main line locomotive would then attach to the 'fulls' and draw them back into siding A and run round the train using line B and headshunt H (after placing a brake van on the rear). Finally it would reattach to the front of the train and, when given the all clear by the signals, draw its train from the sidings, over the crossover between the down and up lines, and head southwards. A light engine, arriving from Alnmouth shed would reverse over the same crossover to gain access to the sidings. Railway company instructions required that sidings A, B, H and J were always empty and available for use by the main line engine. Movements to and from the sidings were under the control of Shilbottle Colliery Sidings signal box which was located on the up side of the main line just to the south of the crossovers and level with sidings J and C.

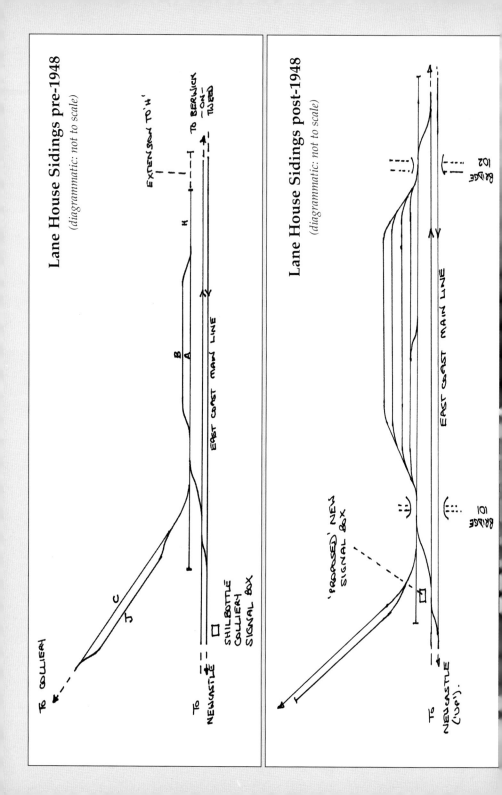

Lane House Sidings pre-1948
(diagrammatic: not to scale)

TO COLLIERY

C
J

TO NEWCASTLE

SHILBOTTLE COLLIERY SIGNAL BOX

B
A

EAST COAST MAIN LINE

H

EXTENSION TO 'H'

TO BERWICK-ON-TWEED

Lane House Sidings post-1948
(diagrammatic: not to scale)

'PROPOSED' NEW SIGNAL BOX

TO NEWCASTLE ('UP').

BRIDGE 101

EAST COAST MAIN LINE

BRIDGE 102

On 4th January, 1927 an agreement came into effect with the North Eastern Railway allowing the Shilbottle Coal Co. to build two sidings on the branch line at Alnwick, to replace the recently closed waggonway as a means of delivering coal to the town for landsale purposes. The two sidings shared the connection to the Alnwick-Alnmouth branch with the Alnwick gas works sidings. The connection was in the form of a trailing crossover from the up line. One of the two sidings was later extended; a weighbridge was located at the entrance to the sidings. The sidings were always worked by engines of the main line companies. Other coal from Shilbottle was hauled to Oxwellmains cement works and to the staithes at the port of Amble, whilst some was sold on site as landsale coal.

By 1948, as traffic had increased, the track formation at Lane House Sidings had been developed considerably. The original loop (composed of sidings C and J) had been removed, and at the former site of lines A and B, five parallel loops were constructed between the underbridges numbered 101 and 102. In addition a trailing crossover had been constructed from these loops to the main line at the northern end, thus allowing coal trains to depart in a northerly direction for the first time. In addition the colliery engine could draw its train of 'fulls' directly into the loops.

Back at the colliery, by 1956 the railway track plan had reached its maximum extent. Starting on the west side of the site there were two sidings with a two-road engine shed and water treatment plant. One siding was located to the side of the stores, iron store and fitting shops. Then there was a siding with a loop which bypassed the screens. There were five roads passing beneath the screens and another siding with a loop bypassing the screens. Finally on the east side there was a siding, with loop, leading to the staithe and landsale yard. There was a weighbridge and weigh house. The screens could deliver coal to the wagons in the following sizes: best coal (4 in. round), cobbles (2½ in.), nuts (1¼ to 2½ inches) and smalls (below 1¼ in.). The maximum permitted load per trip from colliery to Lane House was about 200 tons.

The first steam locomotive to be delivered to Shilbottle was an inside-cylindered 0-6-0 tank locomotive, built by Beyer, Peacock (Works No. 2434) and obtained second-hand after some repairs had been effected by R. & W. Hawthorn, Leslie & Co. It had formerly been the Hull & Barnsley Railway's No. 5 having arrived by May 1923. It performed some useful work at Shilbottle but was subsequently sold or scrapped, perhaps after the third locomotive had arrived. The second locomotive was an outside-cylindered engine 0-4-0 saddle tank obtained new from Peckett's of Bristol (Works No. 1687/1926) carrying the name *Gwen*. This left Shilbottle in 1938, and, after repairs, worked in a Derbyshire Colliery. The third locomotive was another similar Peckett (Works No. 1790/1935) which was named *Olive*. The fourth was an outside-cylindered 0-4-0 saddle tank from Robert Stephenson & Hawthorns Ltd (Works No. 6960/1938). This took on the name of *Gwen* after the first locomotive to carry the name had departed.

The surviving colliery records indicate that early in the pit's history there was only the need for one locomotive to be working at any time, the second locomotive being kept at the colliery as 'spare'. An inventory, made close to the time of nationalization, lists the two locomotives at the 'New Colliery' as:

This NCB internal user metal-bodied side-tipping wagon was one of several used for transporting colliery spoil and other waste to the Shilbottle tip. Others of the same type were found at Whittle where the men referred to them simply as the 'tippers'. They were introduced at both collieries when they opened in the 1920s. *Gordon Hall*

No. 38, RSH 7763/1954, came to Shilbottle from Ashington in October 1969. It is seen here, at Ashington, attached to two high-sided wooden wagons. Note the large headlight fitted on the front of the water tanks. After a brief spell at Whittle the locomotive returned to Shilbottle before ultimate preservation (*see later photographs on pages 45 and 128*). *Author's Collection*

1 saddle tank locomotive by Peckett and Sons; 14″ x 22″ (new 1935)
1 saddle tank locomotive by Stephenson and Hawthorn [*sic*]; 16″ x 24″ (new 1938)

This clearly refers to 1790 and 6960 respectively. These were later numbered 16 and 17 in the NCB North Northumberland Area scheme and had their names removed. These two locomotives shared the work at Shilbottle. Because of their relatively small size they were limited to hauling loads of up to 10 wagons.

Under NCB auspices the former *Olive* left Shilbottle (for repairs at Ashington) by September 1950 and the former *Gwen* had departed by July 1952, also for repairs. It is not certain when either returned to Shilbottle. Both were scrapped sometime in 1964. Other, generally more powerful, steam locomotives to appear at Shilbottle at different times were 0-6-0T locomotives No. 15 (HC1242/1917) and No. 38 (HC1823/1949), also 0-6-0STs No. 5 (P1970/1939), No. 34 (HL2528), No. 27 (RSHN 7178/1944), No. 46 (HE2878/1943), No. 48 (HE 3172/1944), No. 38 (RSH7763/1954) and No. 45 (RSH7113/1943). At the time of maximum coal production, into the 1970s, it became necessary for two steam locomotives to be employed at one time. One locomotive shunted the colliery sidings and serviced the landsale siding whilst the other was engaged in the return trip workings between the colliery and the exchange sidings at the main line. Generally there were six return trips each day, four being during the day shift. The train length on these trips was generally between 15 and 20 wagons though longer trains were hauled from time to time. Trains were operated to the spoil tips using side-tipping wagons. Of all the locomotives that worked at Shilbottle just two are preserved, both at the Tanfield Railway. These are HC1823 and RSH7763 which, by coincidence, had both carried the number 38 whilst at Shilbottle!

In the last years of the colliery's existence several ex-British Railways diesel locomotives (now known as class '08') took over from the steam locomotives. Nos. 52, 55 and 56 (formerly Nos. D4070, D4056 and D4068 respectively) arrived in February 1973, though No. 52 left after about a year. The other two worked at Shilbottle until rail traffic ceased. A diesel hydraulic 0-6-0 loco (EEV D1121) also worked at Shilbottle. At various times these locomotives could be away for repairs or in use at another site.

(Until 1947 pit pony haulage had been used underground. The improvements, gradually effected between 1948 and 1952, transformed the colliery as small locomotives were introduced to move the tubs along a three-mile line from the central loading point to the base of the shaft. These included battery locomotives of 3 ft gauge built by the Logan Mining & Machinery Co. of Dundee (Works Nos. 1976 and 1077 of 1953), and later English Electric locomotive EEV 3845/1968.)

After the underground link was made between Shilbottle and Whittle Drift the surface rail system serving Shilbottle became obsolete. It was closed and the rails were lifted. Today the colliery lies on private land with one of the former colliery buildings converted into a private house. Part of the trackbed forms a public footpath, (an information board having been erected close to the Warkworth-Shilbottle road), but the remainder lies on private land. The mineral-rich spoil tips and water emanating from the former colliery workings are now subject to an EEC-backed scheme for the prevention of water pollution

Locomotive No. 45 was RSH 7113/1945, and was photographed near to the engine shed in the colliery yard at Shilbottle, close by the coal drops and the road vehicle weighbridge. It was owned by the Port of London Authority before coming to the NCB in the North-East at the end of 1960. It worked at Shilbottle from the end of 1963 until May 1968, then, briefly, in January and February 1969. Finally, after a visit to Ashington for repairs, it worked at Shilbottle from April 1969 onwards. After a working life of less than 30 years, it was scrapped in March 1973.

Gordon Hall

Present at Shilbottle engine shed was No. 48, HE 3172/1944 which formerly arrived in Northumberland from the War Department, Bramley, Hampshire. It had two spells at Shilbottle. Whereas many of the NCB working steam locomotives in the county were preserved, No. 48 was unlucky, being scrapped in April 1976.

David Tyreman

by metal waste using beds of reeds. The site of the interchange sidings at Lane House is still discernible though all rails were lifted by the mid-1980s. A public footpath passes near to the site.

4 – *The Whittle Colliery Railway at Newton-on-the-Moor*

The Indenture of 1913 gave Garwood, Paynter & Dunn the go-ahead for the opening of their Drift mine at Whittle. The Shilbottle seam had been thrown upwards by faulting and outcropped in the Whittle area, facilitating access. The seam dipped in an easterly direction at a gradient of about 1 in 3. In addition the Indenture gave them permission to build other tramways and railways as would be needed to carry away the produce of the new pit, or shafts, to a siding on the main line of the NER on the south side of Warkworth station. Before the start of the construction of the Whittle Drift in the second decade of the 20th century, there had only been one small mine shaft at Whittle, located just below the house known as Low Newton. This mine may have been associated with the burning of lime at Whittle limestone quarry a few hundred yards to the east.

When the new drift to the east of the Hampeth Burn was opened by the South Shilbottle Co. towards the end of World War I, a narrow gauge tramway was laid. This linked the drift, the old mine shaft and an adjacent quarry (where there were several sidings, perhaps for wagon storage), with two staithes which were used for the loading of road vehicles. At this time the colliery was wholly landsale, providing coal for household purposes. The tramway line involved the use of some very sharp curves. The details are shown on the 1921 Ordnance Survey map. It is assumed that horses were used to work the line.

Construction of the link between the Whittle Drift and the East Coast Main Line was started slightly after the start of construction of the Shilbottle link to the same line. The start of works does not appear on the 1921 maps though, as the first locomotive was delivered in 1924, it must have started soon afterwards and proceeded rapidly. Its total track length was about five miles if the length of track in sidings is included. It was laid with bull-head rails in chairs attached to wooden sleepers.

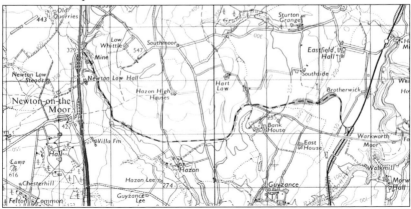

The NCB Whittle Colliery line.   *Ordnance Survey, Crown Copyright, all rights reserved*

A delightful picture of the Whittle Colliery ambulance taken soon after the rail-served pit opened. In the background on the right are some wooden-sided, former NER hopper wagons. It was necessary to digitally enhance the poor quality original photograph.   *Author's Collection*

So as to equalize flange wear local NCB locomotives were permitted to traverse the British Railways branch to Alnwick so that they could be turned on the station turntable. Here *Bella*, Peckett 1628/1924, which was Whittle Colliery's first locomotive, avails itself of this facility.

John Mallon, Beamish Museum Collection

The line left the colliery site heading in a southerly, then south-easterly direction, above the line of the Hampeth Burn and its junction with the Hazon Burn. Along this section the line descended fairly gently. It passed the site of the old shaft and curved towards the east and south-east, following the line of the burn. It then left the course of the burn and headed due eastwards, crossing firstly the minor road between Hazon and Hazon High Houses and then a second road to the east of Hazon. Here the line climbed quite steeply in the direction of Bank House. On crossing the Westwood Burn the line headed northwards, then north-eastwards, crossing the Quarry Burn before passing through a small wood, and over another level crossing just to the north of Bank House. After this summit the line started to descend, crossing several fields in a shallow cutting. Having initially begun to swing north the line then made a sharp curve towards the east, then south, before yet another level crossing, this time over the minor, lightly-used road, to the south of Brotherwick. Just a short distance later the line arrived at the 'Southside interchange sidings' by the main line, about halfway between Warkworth and Acklington stations. 'Southside' was the name of a farm located about half a mile away to the north-west. The line had descended nearly 130 ft between the Quarry Burn and the interchange sidings, a gradient that was often to pose difficulties in the braking of trains of loaded wagons and in the return of the empties to the colliery!

At Southside there were originally three sidings, later increased to six as traffic increased. Late in the life of the line another two sidings were laid but these were never used. A wagon weighbridge was, in later years, located in the sidings at Southside.

The first locomotive to be delivered to Whittle was an outside-cylindered Peckett 0-4-0 saddle tank (Works No. 1628) delivered in 1924. It carried the name *Bella*. The second locomotive was another 0-4-0 saddle tank, also with outside cylinders, this time a R. & W. Hawthorn (Works No. HL3741/1930) which carried the name *Ivy*. Both of these locomotives were bought new from their manufacturers. These two locomotives handled the traffic at Whittle until the colliery passed into NCB ownership after World War II, and for some time afterwards.

In the 1947 inventory they were described as:

1 4-wheel loco no. 3741 by Hawthorne Leslie [*sic*], Newcastle. 12" diameter cylinders, 14" stroke; 23 tons weight. Built 1930; purchased 1930.
1 4-wheel loco no. 1628 by Peckett and Sons, Bristol. Built 1924. 14" cylinders, 20" stroke. New boiler fitted to the above, complete with tubes, fittings and firebox.

Both locomotives ceased to work at Whittle in the mid-1960s, their replacements being much larger six-wheeled locomotives. These included No. 52 (a Bagnall-built 'Austerity', Works No. 2780/1945), No. 51 (Bagnall 2757/1944), No. 26 (Vulcan Foundry-built 5278/1945, fitted with a Giesl ejector) and No. 44 (RSH 7104/1943, also Giesl-fitted). Some of these were in poor condition and Nos. 52 and 26 soon needed attention at Ashington workshops. No. 29 (RSH side-tank 7607/1950) arrived as a replacement for No. 52 and No. 27 (RSH 7178/1944) arrived to replace No. 26. Later, No. 33 (VF 5306/1945) and No. 31 (RSH 7609/1950) arrived to solve motive power crises. At the end of 1969

No. 19, formerly named *Ivy*, was the second locomotive purchased for Whittle Colliery by the Cooperative Wholesale Society. It arrived new as works number HL3741/1930 and entered into NCB ownership at nationalization. It was ultimately replaced by more powerful locomotives and, after a period out-of-use in 'The Heap Road', was scrapped in January 1967.

Beamish Museum Collection

Richard, outside-cylindered 0-4-0 saddle tank, Peckett 2054 of 1944, arrived at Whittle in 1964 after repairs at Seaton Delaval workshops. It performed little work at Whittle and is shown here standing at the top of 'The Heap Road' in the mid-1960s, still bearing its nameplates. It was scrapped in 1968. *Beamish Museum Collection*

there were five locomotives at Whittle: Nos. 31 and 33 were in regular use, No. 44 was spare engine, whilst Nos. 27 and 51 were out-of-use, the last laid-up, without its coupling rods, awaiting attention. In 1970 Whittle received No. 38 (RSH 7763/1954) from nearby Shilbottle. To replace engines leaving Whittle No. 47 (RSH 7849/1955) arrived in 1971 though it struggled to work trains on the line to Southside. Of these locomotives, both Nos. 31 and 47 were saved for preservation by the North Yorkshire Moors Railway. Subsequently No. 47 moved to the Lincolnshire Wolds Railway whilst No. 31 was transferred to the Avon Valley Railway located at Oldland Common, between Bath and Bristol.

No shed was ever provided for the steam locomotives at Whittle, and there was no inspection pit. There was no specialist coaling point, the engines being filled beneath the washer. Maintenance was thus always a problem.

As at Shilbottle, the last years of the Whittle system saw the employment of diesel locomotives on the trains. A small shed was provided for these adjacent to one of the pit's airshafts. This two-road building had an inspection pit and a locomen's bothy nearby. Diesels were at first hired-in from British Railways, Gateshead depot normally supplying them. Later, in 1972-73 the NCB supplied some locomotives of its own including NCB 51 (formerly BR D4069), NCB 53 (D4072) and NCB 54 (D4074). Later arrivals still were 52 (D4070), which had also worked at Shilbottle, and then 56 (D4068) which replaced 52. Other Whittle-based diesels included EEV D1121/1966, Barclay 647/1979, diesel-hydraulic 64 (NBL 27763/1959) and 510/1 (former early-BR diesels 12029 and 12133 built at Darlington in 1952). Barclay 647 is known to have struggled to cope with the work at Whittle. Other locomotives known to have spent a brief time at Whittle include Andrew Barclay-built 0-6-0 diesel-hydraulics with works numbers AB582, 584, 613, and 615. Finally, in the last years of NCB operation, various 0-6-0 diesels of class '08' were 'hired in' from British Rail including Nos. D3182, D3215, D3875 and D3934.

Whereas in the early days at Shilbottle just one locomotive could cope with the work, at Whittle two were in daily use. One job was confined to the immediate colliery area and was thus known as the 'Short Run', whilst the trips along the full length of the line to Southside were known as the 'Long Run'. The former could be performed by a locomotive which was slightly underpowered (such as the Barclay diesels in later years) whilst the latter required a locomotive in top condition on account of the loads and gradients involved. Whereas Shilbottle had used locomotives underground to move the coal in tubs, at Whittle the coal was moved by conveyor to the drift entrance and taken to the screens in standard gauge wagons. The 'short run' involved placing the wagons at the screens so that they could run, by gravity, to the loading bunker where they were moved by an endless rope system. There were, at the time of nationalization, four roads beneath the screens. (The Avery weighing machine at the colliery was later declared redundant and replaced by one at Southside.) The 'short run' job also involved moving wagons to and from the landsale siding where coal was dropped from hoppers onto a belt which fed a hopper from which road lorries were loaded. For a time when the underground link was being constructed between Shilbottle and Whittle the run also involved collection of waste stone from the drift mouth ready for taking down to

No. 33 (VF5306/1945) pauses at Bankhouse Crossing for the shunter to pin down some of the wagon brakes to assist the locomotive brakes on the 1½ mile downhill gradient. This particular working could consist of up to 10 16-ton mineral wagons and 10 20-ton hoppers, all 'fulls', a possible total load of about 360 tons.   *Cliff Shepherd*

The period is the late 1960s as No. 44 (RSH 7104/1943), fitted with a Giesl ejector, hauls four full hopper wagons from the drift to the screens for the coal to be sorted. Four was the usual number of wagons for this operation. On the right is the 2 ft gauge track which carried men to and from the drift.   *Ken Middlemist Collection*

No. 31 ((RSH7609/1950) passes the flower-covered tip as it drifts down to shunt wagons in the screen roads at Whittle Colliery. On the right are hopper wagons in the landsale siding. If internal-user wagons were in short supply hoppers from the main line companies were 'borrowed' to move landsale coal within the yard! The 'Keeker's Office' (the foreman's office) and staff cars are in the background in this 1960s scene. *Gordon Hall*

One of the Ruston & Hornsby diesel locomotives runs on its 2 ft gauge tracks near some standard gauge NCB internal-user hopper wagons standing on the 'main loop' line at Whittle. These 'hoppers' were used to move coal to the screens, or coal from the screens to the landsale siding. The narrow gauge lines were known at the pit as 'the rolleyway' and its small "tub" wagons, some of which are shown in the foreground, were used for transporting supplies, tools, wood and other materials. *Gordon Hall*

No. 31 (RSH7609/1950) arrived at Whittle from Ashington in May 1969. Here, in the hands of driver Fred Wilkinson, it is passing the colliery air shaft on its way with laden hoppers from the drift to the screens. This locomotive passed into preservation with the North Yorkshire Moors Railway in March 1973.
Cliff Shepherd

The year is 1985 and driver Ken Middlemist uses a Barclay diesel to propel a train of empty British Rail wagons towards the screens. There were four screen roads: for 'best', 'cobbles', 'doubles' and 'small' coal. The buildings to the left of the locomotive were the electricians', fitters' and blacksmith's shops.
Ken Middlemist Collection

Widdrington where it was used to fill in some spent opencast pits. The loads on the 'short run' rarely exceeded about four wagons. For delivery of coal to the landsale yard some 'internal user' wooden-sided hoppers were used; these had been described in the 1947 inventory as '3 railway waggons of 20 ton and 1 waggon of 8 ton' [sic].

The 'long run' involved taking wagonloads of screened and washed coal from the colliery to Southside. The screens at Whittle sorted the coal into best coal, cobbles, doubles (or 'nuts') and small coal. The run also included collecting and taking to Southside any wagons of stone from the construction of the new underground roadway. Loaded trains were usually up to about 400 tons but occasionally loadings reached almost 500 tons. The downhill length from Bank House to Southside required the shunter to pin down wagon brakes, those on every alternate wagon normally being sufficient, though there are some tales of near-accidents when trains found it difficult to stop, especially when rails were wet! The return journey up the gradient, especially on wet days, required a good fire, a boiler full of steam and much effort from the 0-6-0 locomotive when taking a load of about 20 'empties' back to the colliery. The loads taken to and from the main line by the original 0-4-0 saddle tanks appear not to have been recorded.

Whittle also had a second surface railway system of two feet gauge for moving materials. This used several Ruston & Hornsby diesel-mechanical locomotives including Nos. RH268866, RH268862 and RH393979, plus a fourth from Hudswell, Clarke (HC DM 842). Two Clayton 4-wheeled battery electric locomotives CE B0451 and B1539 completed the roster.

A 2 ft narrow gauge system, largely underground, employed several English Electric 4-wheeled battery electric locomotives, recharged between periods of usage, for conveying men to and from the drift and pit head baths, also for transporting materials. These locomotives included EE 2420, 2474, 2527, 2635, 2638, 2696 and 3404. Nos. EE 2474 and 2527 were left underground at the closure of the mine and were taken over by ERS Mining (see below). (Fuller details of all of the surface and underground locomotives, including their dates of arrival and departure from both Whittle and Shilbottle collieries can be found in the Handbook Industrial Locomotives of Northumberland published by the Industrial Railway Society; a new edition is in preparation.)

With the merger of the Shilbottle and Whittle pits in 1982 a decision was made to install shearer faces in the pit instead of working the coal by hand. However, the smallest shearer drums available were of 34 inches depth. The seam at the combined pit was just 28 inches deep and so six inches of rock would have been mixed with the coal! This would have seriously affected the quality of the coal and hence the price obtained. A financially unviable pit was the inevitable consequence. Closure of the pit was announced in March 1987 and hundreds of jobs were lost. The railway was closed and the rails soon lifted. However, a few years afterwards coal mining returned to Whittle when a concern called ERS Mining Developments (NE) Ltd, reopened the Whittle Pit. They employed a 2 ft gauge surface railway system using two small locomotives. The first was a 4-wheeled battery-electric machine, built by Wingrove & Rogers in Liverpool (WR6299/1960). This locomotive had formerly worked in Weardale for BRM

Driver Ken Middlemist of Hipsburn stands proudly next to No. 51, his former British Rail, Darlington-built, class '08' shunter (ex-D4069) at Southside Sidings adjacent to the East Coast main line. His shunter, George Briggs, is out of the picture attending to the wagons!

National Coal Board, Ken Middlemist Collection

Industries. The second locomotive was a 4-wheeled diesel-mechanical machine 104C063/1976 built by Simplex Mechanical Handling at Bedford, this firm being the successor to Motor Rail. This locomotive was supplied by Alan Keef Ltd of Lea Link, Ross-on-Wye. The locomotives could be seen working between the drift entrance and the mine buildings close to the A1. This was the last firm to run a railway at the Whittle site.

In February 2008 the BBC's local 'Text' service stated that Whittle Mine was to be auctioned in May 2008. Apparently three companies were showing interest in the site. The guide price was £4 million! Permission would be included to mine coal until 2019. In late 2009 some portable two-storey staff accommodation had been erected (without planning permission apparently) for a possible resumption of mining.

Today the Whittle site, viewed 'over the fence' from the adjacent A1 road, looks somewhat 'untidy', especially so with the erection of the portable buildings. Some private artificial lakes have been constructed for anglers to the south of the colliery site. The trackbed of the railway remains, marked as 'dismantled railway' on OS maps, though most of it crosses private land. However, it can be seen from public footpaths which cross it at various points including to the west of Hazon High Houses and near Southside Farm. Additional viewing points include the various former level crossings. A public footpath parallels the trackbed on the gradient between Hazon and Bank House. The site of Southside sidings can be viewed from the road over the East Coast main line on Warkworth Moor south of Brotherwick. Southside signal box has long since disappeared.

The final photograph in this chapter illustrates RSH 7763, built as late as 1954, which worked at Shilbottle before transfer to Whittle. After another 20 months it moved back to Shilbottle for the rest of its NCB career. It is shown here in preservation hauling a three-coach passenger train at The Tanfield Railway in August 1986. Marley Hill locoshed is in the background.   *Author*

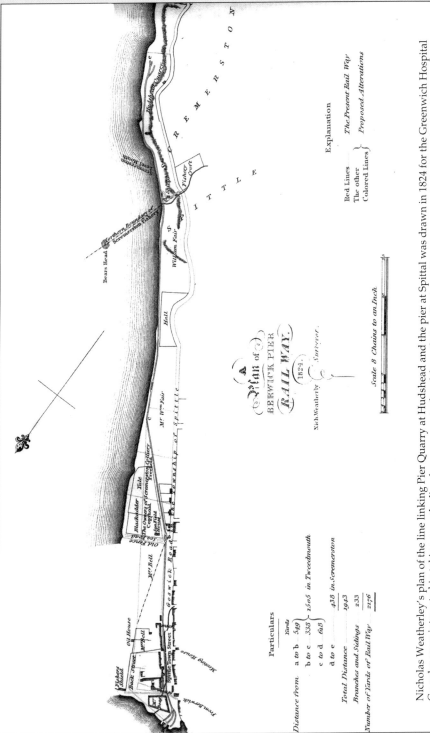

Nicholas Weatherley's plan of the line linking Pier Quarry at Hudshead and the pier at Spittal was drawn in 1824 for the Greenwich Hospital Co. who were interested in taking over the line for movement of coal from their collieries at Scremerston to the harbour for loading onto sea-going vessels.

Chapter Four

The Colliery Railways
of the Berwick Coalfield

5 – The Spittal Railway

The Spittal Railway (or 'Spittal Tramroad') was constructed towards the end of the first decade of the 19th century. Although it was constructed for carrying stone, it became, later in an extended form, a coal-carrying line linking the collieries at Scremerston with the mouth of the Tweed.

Whilst there had been a pier at the mouth of the Tweed at Spittal from 1768, the harbour facilities there had been regarded as inadequate for many years. The Harbour Commissioners decided that there was a need for improvements and a Bill (Bill 47, George 3rd 1806-7) was presented by Sir John Callender to Parliament on 26th March, 1807. The Act was duly passed and was given the Royal Assent on 10th June, 1808. The Act authorized the carrying of stone, sand, gravel and clay from quarries and pits to the site and allowed the building of necessary roads, ways and passages to aid construction. The stone was to be

This picture postcard, entitled 'The Cliffs, Spittal' [sic], shows Huds Head which is located just outside the Spittal boundary in Scremerston parish; the Pier Quarry is hidden just behind this. The Spittal Railway followed a line close to the upper limits of the beach. Some of the rocks beneath Huds Head still show evidence of the rail fastenings. The later coal line from Scremerston's Restoration Pit descended the cliffs on a steep incline.   *Author's Collection*

The visit of George IV to Berwick is commemorated in the painting by Robert Good. The Spittal Railway is shown with a horse-drawn wagon. Some artistic licence is employed as both the Berwick Castle (demolished on the arrival of the railway) and the Royal Border Bridge appear in the same view!   *Berwick Museum and Art Gallery*

obtained from a clifftop quarry in a field known as 'Huds Head' further south down the coast from Spittal and '…it was considered advisable to make a railway for conveying stone from the Quarry to the intended Pier…' This quarry was variously known as Hudshead Quarry or Pier Quarry. The Pier was to be constructed at Carr Rock.

Although much of the line followed the streets of Spittal it was necessary for the commissioners to purchase some private land to complete the project. For example in May 1810 William and Margaret Fair agreed to 'The Release of a Piece of [their] Ground at Spittle [sic] for an Iron Rail Road'.

The Pier Quarry at Huds Head, by the cliffs south of Spittal, was already opened and working in March 1809 when the Harbour Commissioners advertised for estimates for ironwork associated with the building of the line. Estimates were to be received at the Town Hall in Berwick no later than 10th April, 1809: 'Ironwork to be supplied for a line from Hudshead Quarry (now working) to Spittle [sic] being a distance of 1,700 yards.' One-third of the iron work was to be delivered on or before 1st May, 1810, the second third by 15th May, 1810 and the final third before the end of the same month. Several estimates were received but the one that was accepted was from John Robertson and company of 'Berwick Foundry' (actually the Tower Foundry in Tweedmouth). John Robertson was one of the Harbour Commissioners! Robertson agreed to deliver the rails on Spittal Sands at a cost of £11 8s. 0d. per ton, '… the Rails not exceeding 40 lb. nor below 38 lb. per yard'. The foundry also agreed to supply other unspecified metal articles, perhaps rail fastenings. Tracklaying proceeded rapidly and the necessary stone was soon being brought down from the quarry. (The foundation stone for the new pier had actually been laid on 27th February, 1810. After a short ceremony a dinner was held at the Hen and Chicken Inn at 4 pm.)

The early days of the line were not without incident. On 27th May, 1811 a small child, playing on the railway at Spittal, was knocked down by a wagon and bruised so badly that at the time it was considered that there was little hope of the child's survival. The event was reported in the local newspaper of 1st June. The line was gravity-worked for the first part of its length and wagons may have developed a good speed when descending the gradient from the quarry. The remainder of the line was horse-worked, as was the return of the wagons to the quarry.

Although contemporary documents use both the terms 'plates' and rails', most use the former term and it is almost certain that the original line was, in fact, a plateway, that is with flangeless wagon wheels running on L-shaped plates.

The weight and speed of the wagons may have contributed to the considerable breakage of the 'rail plates' supplied by Robertson's. A complaint was made to the company in 1811 and replacements were supplied. However, these proved to be of no better quality than the original ones. The Harbour Commissioners contemplated taking Robertson to court over the matter and a Barrister was briefed. They had arranged for an inspector, Mr Fox, to examine the broken items and, following his Report, they sent for Robert Guthrie, one of the foundry partners. Guthrie admitted that some of the plates had been made of inferior metal and agreed a 5 per cent discount off the outstanding account.

He agreed to allow £6 per ton for broken plates returned and agreed to supply new plates for one year at a price of £13 15s. 0d. per ton, with a discount of 5 per cent on prompt settlement of the account. This was accepted by the Commissioners at their next meeting on the condition that the new plates were of the required quality. However, the new plates delivered were of such inferior quality that the rate of breakage actually increased! In 1813 the cost of replacing plates exceeded the cost that might have been expected in relaying the whole railway. The Commissioners resisted paying for the replacement plates. Also they refused to return all of the damaged plates as they would be required as evidence in litigation. William Chapman, an eminent engineer from Newcastle, was engaged by the Commissioners to examine 'the Road'. He visited the line on 23rd July, 1813 and presented his report the following day.

In this report he identified the usual causes of breakages as being caused by, '... uncommon quickness in motion of the vehicles, deficiency of the size of the track in relation to the weight carried over it, imperfect setting of the rails on stones which are liable to sink unequally, and the use of metal unfit for the purpose'.

His findings were that the first two of these could not have been the cause. He considered that the stability of the stone sleepers may have contributed as they were laid on sand, the ends of the rails being laid on the stones. His suggested remedy was to replace the sand with a bed of chalk, rubbish and engine ash of 9 in. thickness under the base of the stones and extending around them. All should then be beaten with a paviours hammer to effect consolidation.

Remains of the sleeper blocks from the Spittal Railway exist, either in private ownership or public collections. These sleeper blocks are in the Berwick Museum Collection.
Berwick Museum and Art Gallery

Chapman made several recommendations:

Obtain iron plates to the same specification from another foundry
Relay 10 yards in each 100 yards at 90 yard intervals with this new rail
Some of the heavier-than-usual-stones carried over the way should be recarried over the way
A daily record should be taken of the stones carried over the way and the number of rails broken
A comparison of the strength of the existing plates with the new ones should be made
The broken rails should be replaced with similar new ones and thence the breakage per 1,000 tons of stone taken over them should be ascertained
Only then should the account be settled with the iron company.

The Commissioners obtained some new 'rails' from the Newcastle Foundry and laid them as recommended. The rails supplied from Newcastle were found to have a weight of 115 lb. i.e. approximately 39 lb. per yard but the replacements supplied by Robertson for the test weighed in at 131 lb. per yard (i.e. 44 lb. per yard, well over the specification!). A scientific test was conducted using '...a given leaver...' and it was found that Robertson's plates broke at an average of 226 lb. whilst those from Newcastle broke at a weight of 382 lb., that is, the Newcastle ones were 44 per cent stronger. This showed that Robertson's materials were contrary to the contract and the company was accused of deliberately hiding the strength and quality of his metals by making them a full 6 lb. heavier! The Commissioners reported additional expenses as a result of their wagons (especially the wheels) being destroyed, the costs of necessary additional workmanship in replacing the plates and repairing the road, costs in having to unload and reload wagons, and the effect of all of this on the stoppage of harbour works. All of this formed part of the Commissioners case being prepared for court by James Bullock of Gray's Inn, London in November 1813 when Robertson sought payment of unpaid monies. The matter was finally settled in the Commissioners' favour and stone was moved over the line until the pier was completed.

Sleeper blocks with the remains of plate-rails from the Spittal Railway in the Berwick Museum Collection.   *Berwick Museum and Art Gallery*

After a few years of disuse the line was reopened, but not for carrying stone. It would appear that the lessees of the Scremerston Colliery from the Greenwich Hospital Estate, who owned the site, were making use of the line to transport coal to the jetty for loading onto sea-going vessels. Initially this appears to have been done without permission. In a later legal case this movement of coal along the line was considered to have been 'improper'. The line at this time was probably still a plateway as it is unlikely that the new users would have relaid the line as a true railway until they had regularized their use of it.

However, on 27th July, 1819 Joseph Forster and Thomas Wallis on behalf of the 'Receivers of Greenwich Hospital' replied to a letter from the Harbour Commissioners regarding the purchase of the 'Right of Passage' along the Rail Road at Spittle [*sic*] from the hospital estate at Scremerston to the River Tweed. Documentation is incomplete but the Commissioners invited the Greenwich estate to make an offer for the railway, though certain conditions were attached. The sale appears not to have taken place until the 1820s.

Eventually the Greenwich Hospital estates had the entire route surveyed in detail by Nicholas Weatherley (along with the rest of their local estate lands).

This engraving is taken from a sale bill and shows 'The Shipping Place of Greenwich Hospital Coals'. Towards the right is the Old Berwick bridge and in the centre the church at Tweedmouth. At the head of the train on the left is a locomotive with a large chimney. Was this the 'Puffing Billy-type' locomotive to which Mr Carr, the later colliery Director, referred in 1931?   *Berwick Museum Collection*

Fortunately his map, dated 1824, entitled *The Berwick Pier Railway* survives in a collection in the Northumberland Archives at Woodhorn. The line is shown, on this map, as starting at the quarry at Hudshead where three sidings are shown. A building, which may have been connected with the quarry, was located directly opposite the nearby road. The line of railway then followed the coastline very closely before arriving at the first passing loop at Shields. This was located 438 yards from the quarry. The line crossed from Scremerston into Tweedmouth at this point. It continued another 618 yards, across the land of Mr William Fair, to the second passing loop. After a further 338 yards there was the third passing loop, shortly after the line left the coastline and headed inland towards what is now Spittal High Street. In those days this part of the road was known as 'Goswick Road'. It passed along Goswick Road and continued into 'Spittle Town Street' before arriving at its jetty terminus, some 549 yards from

The alignment of the Spittal Railway followed what is now South Greenwich Road en route from the Hudshead Quarry and seafront to the Spittal High Street. This house, in the fork of the two roads, retains a 'wedge shape'. *Inset:* South Greenwich Road sign. This road is named after the Greenwich Hospital which started to operate the collieries and the railway from Scremerston in the mid-19th century.   *(Both) Author*

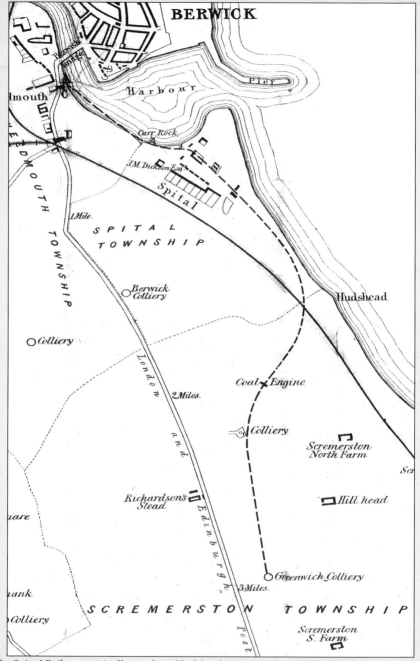

The Spittal Railway originally ran from Hudshead to near to Carr Rock. After the connection of the Greenwich Colliery at Scremerston to the Spittal Railway, an 1840s extension was planned to take the line beyond the Carr Rocks to a new terminus close to Berwick Old bridge. In the event this extension was not proceeded with as the collieries started to dispatch their coal via a link with the newly-constructed Newcastle & Berwick Railway (*shown here as the solid black line running parallel with the coastline*).   *Berwick-on-Tweed Record Office*

the previous loop. Here the map indicates the existence of three sidings on the Jetty, one possessing a further passing loop. The total length of the line was stated to be 1,943 yards plus a further 233 yards as 'branches and sidings'.

Other printed maps exist in the same folder. One, showing the Scremerston estate to the south but including part of the line, indicates just two sidings in the Hudshead Quarry. On this, and other maps, there are pencil lines which link the colliery, near to Scremerston, with points on the railway route in the direction of Spittal. In addition an 'engine' is marked at a location called 'colliery ground'. Developments were obviously afoot!

Rule's Map, also dated 1824 but presumably surveyed slightly later than Weatherley's, shows the route of the southerly part of the line leading towards the collieries at Scremerston, with an engine house constructed at the head of a new, steep inclined plane leading the line up towards the colliery. The section of the line into the Pier Quarry at Huds Head is not shown and presumably, therefore, had been abandoned. It is quite possible that this was the time when the plateway was converted to a railway on a new alignment as all subsequent documents refer to the line as a 'railway' or a 'tramway'.

Until this time the coal would have emanated from the colliery known as Scremerston Old Pit (variously known as Old Restoration Pit, Colliery Ground Pit or simply the Scremerston Colliery). It was located on land formerly part of Borewell Farm and linked by means of a cartway to the Great North Road. This may indicate that some landsale of coal took place. The new railway probably served the recently sunk Restoration Pit nearby. On the new railway horses moved the coal-filled wagons to the top of the incline where a rope was attached allowing a controlled lowering of the wagons by gravity. The wagons on the new line joined the route of the former stone railway as it reached the lower end of its descent into Spittal, probably, in view of the gradients, with further gravity assistance. On reaching street level it was necessary to reattach a horse for the wagons to be pulled through Spittal to the jetty. The line joined Town Street at an acute angle and followed the centre of this road towards the Coastguard station and Lifeboat House. During the passage along Town Street a siding was created which trailed in from the west (see later). The wagons were then hauled onwards to the jetty where there was a crane to assist with the loading of vessels. (An 1822 painting by Good, depicting the visit of George IV to Berwick, shows, at one side, the line with a chaldron wagon being hauled by a horse along stone-sleepered track close to the sea shore at Spittal.) Empties were returned to the bottom of the incline by horses. They were then hauled to the top of the incline using the newly-erected steam engine and winch located in the engine house near its top. Rule's map omits any details of passing loops on the 'new' line.

As suggested above, the early 1820s saw the closure of the 'Old Pit'. A new shaft was sunk not far away. This was known as the 'Restoration Pit' (otherwise as 'Old Hill Pit' or simply 'Scremerston Colliery') at NU008495 on later Ordnance maps. The first lease on this Pit was granted on 11th January, 1824 for a period of 21 years. The lessee in the 1820s was Robert Johnson (who may, or may not, have been the 'Major Johnstone' known to have operated another pit in the Scremerston area in the early 1800s). Records show that some 1,218

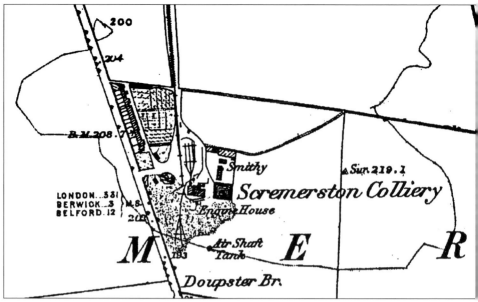

The second Scremerston Colliery was situated to the east of the Great North Road exactly three miles away from Berwick. Its rail connection headed north, passing close to the site of the first Scremerston pit (Restoration Pit), before reaching the head of the cable-worked incline leading to the exchange sidings for the East Coast main line.

The third rail-connected colliery at Scremerston was to the west of the original Great North Road. This 1905 view shows the colliery pit head with wagons being loaded beneath the screens. To the left is the Scremerston Brick & Tile Works which possessed its own narrow-gauge tramway system.   *Author's Collection*

imperial chaldrons of coal were shipped from the Pier in 1828 (though some of this may have come along the Unthank line – *see later*). By 1833 the company operating the colliery, then known as Robert Johnson and Co., planned to increase by a further four the number of ships (then around 12-13) operating from the mouth of the Tweed.

The Harbour Commissioners clearly retained the ownership of most of the line throughout the 1820s though by 1830 the Commissioners of Greenwich Hospital had renewed their interest in the line applying for an Act, which was granted, to extend the line northwards from '...near the school house in Spital [*sic*] and to terminate at or near the south end of the bridge across the River Tweed situate in Tweedmouth ... and to make an maintain the said railway and works'. The Act specified the right to build inclined planes, embankments, walls, aqueducts, bridges, roadways, passages, drains, cuttings and fences. It also gave the Commissioners leave to grant leases of coal or minerals for '42 years...from the 10th year of King George IVth'. Plans and sections of the proposed railway were lodged with the Clerk of the Peace for Berwick. It is doubtful whether the developments were actually effected for by 1835 the Scremerston Colliery, then in a detached part of County Durham, was being advertised for sale (along with some limeworks and a farm) in the local newspapers.

> *SALE NOTICE: Sale of Colliery, Lime Works etc. in North Durham.*
> All that valuable current-going LAND-SALE and SEA-SALE COLLIERY known by the name of SCREMERSTON COLLIERY situate at Scremerston, near Berwick-upon-Tweed ... landsale at this colliery is considerable and the Spital [*sic*] Railway with inclined planes, wagons, boxes etc are sufficient for a sea vend of 20,000 tons annually. At an outlay of a few hundred pounds the shipping place at Spital may be made suitable for vessels of 15 feet draught water, the railway from the colliery to the river being one mile and three quarters in length. A convenient coal depot in Berwick, two cranes and two keels belong to the Colliery ... [are also available].

However, the colliery was to close completely within the next five years! It is quite possible that the railway fell out of use for a period in the 1830s as the fortunes of the colliery had declined. A contemporary plan associated with the building of the Newcastle & Berwick main line railway marks the Spittal line as 'Old Colliery Railway', for example.

By 1840 a new colliery was sunk at Scremerston down to the Blackhill seam. It is usually reported that the 'Carr Brothers' were responsible for its sinking, though the first Lessees are recorded as Messrs Johnson and Carr. The colliery was located at Richardson's Stead to the south of the previous two Scremerston collieries (NU010484). The colliery was usually known as Greenwich Colliery though it has also been referred to as 'Scremerston New Winning', 'Scremerston New Colliery', 'Jack Tar Pit', 'Jack Tar Colliery' or simply 'Scremerston Colliery'. After closure it was referred to as Scremerston Old Colliery also. A newspaper report (in the *Berwick Advertiser*) referred to the '...owners, or reputed owners...' as being the Commissioners of Greenwich Hospital. This 'doubt' may arise from the splitting of the former estate lands between the Parishes of Tweedmouth and Ancroft in about 1835. The lessees consisted of a consortium consisting of Robert Johnson and his wife, five members of the Carr family, a Martin Morrison and his wife, John Grey and Thomas Cargill. The consortium was reconstituted in 1850

This photograph of the colliery sidings at the third Scremerston Colliery shows empty wooden-sided wagons awaiting loading at the screens. Some earlier 'chaldron' wagons stand in front of the colliery buildings. These were used for removal of spoil including clay.　*Author's Collection*

The Robert Stephenson-built tank locomotive RS2841, built in 1896, came to Scremerston in 1935 from the Hartley Main Collieries and worked there until the pit closed in 1944. It replaced two earlier locomotives, one built by Andrew Barclay and the other by Manning, Wardle. Photographs of these two locomotives have proved to be elusive!　*Henderson Family Collection*

and traded as the Scremerston and Shoreswood Colliery Company until around the time of the closure of this colliery in May 1878.
  In 1843 it was the intention of,

> ...the Commissioners of Greenwich Hospital to repair the *railway* ... [author's italics] ... through the Main Street of Spittal for the purpose of conveying coals from Scremerston New Colliery to the Jetty.' An Act was also drawn up for the Commissioners '...for Making and Repairing a Railway or Tramway from Spittal to near to the South End of Berwick Bridge between high and low water.' The Act actually covered the making of a new line from the location described as 'Schoolhouse' at Spittal to Berwick Bridge. The new line would have involved the compulsory purchase of necessary land in Tweedmouth and close to the bridge. Plans and sections were included in the Act. In 1845 a separate Act was put together '...to enable the Commissioners of Greenwich Hospital to grant Leases of Coal and Minerals for 42 years and also to make a *railway* ... [author's italics] ...from the Schoolhouse in Spittal to Berwick Bridge'.

This extension to the railway, similar to that planned in 1830, would have been about ½ mile in length.
  There was considerable objection voiced against the proposed Act. The proprietors of nearby Berwick Hill Colliery (John Paxton and Richard Reavely) objected on the grounds that the line would help create a monopoly for Scremerston Colliery. The Duke of Northumberland objected as did the Berwick Harbour Commissioners. Owners of land to be crossed by the proposed line also objected; such included the Berwick Shipping Company. William Whitehouse, a Minister of the Church, objected on behalf of the people of Spittal saying that the existing line had not been operated in a safe manner, that the line running down the Main Street was a source of danger and that three children had died having been overrun by wagons. One of these is likely to have been the child killed in the 1811 accident. The line's second accident happened on 11th May, 1832 when the 11-year-old son of a pitman called Robert Barnes was killed after he tripped over the rails and was run over. It has not been possible to trace details of a third accident on the railway, though one pitman's daughter, Catherine Smart, was killed at the colliery when she tripped and was strangled between a cable being used to raise tubs and a winding drum. She was running to deliver her father's dinner at the time.
  The Greenwich Hospital's plan was that the best coals would go for export but the inferior coals could be sold to home consumers at a cheaper rate. They were prepared to allow the lessees of the Borough's small colliery (precise location not discovered) to move coal along their line at a favourable rate. In the event the extension to the line was not built for an 1852 Board of Health map shows it terminating at Spittal Jetty, not near to Berwick bridge. J.E. Carr, in 1931, reported that '... rather than being built as planned, the existing coal and pier tramroads were adapted, and continued to terminate at the three jetties close to Ellstell Fishery, Spittal ...' The Health Board map confirms one jetty as having two faces, then there was a loading area, then another jetty with a crane, then a 'basin' then another pier. The line, on this map, ran along 'Front Street', past the 'Herring Stores', between the 'Sheep Inn' and 'The Golden Fleece' and had a double-tracked section past the 'Salmon Inn' as far as 'Spital Post Office'. A short branch ran to the south-west, curving between two buildings into

Above: Scremerston incline connected the pits in the Scremerston area with, initially, the wagonway to Spittal, and later the exchange sidings with the Newcastle & Berwick Railway. A Kings Cross to Edinburgh train passes the foot of the incline in January 2011.

Author

Right: On this stone sleeper block can be made out the imprint of a rail chair. Several of these blocks can be found on the Scremerston Incline below where the colliery line made a level crossing with the road leading to Cocklawburn beach.

Author

Middle Street, where it terminated next to a corn mill. Perhaps corn or flour was also transported along this part of the line to or from the jetties. The line, on its way back to the colliery, ran past the 'St Helen's Foundry' and diverted towards the shore at 'Blenheim Place'.

Mr Carr also related that in the early 1840s coal was being exported from Berwick to Amsterdam, Bordeaux, Rouen and other continental ports. Vessels of up to 450 tons were in use for this traffic. In 1855, for example, 8,285 tons of coal left Berwick in this way. Other coals were sent to Harwich, London and Folkestone.

The story of the lower part of the line was about to come to an end, its fate sealed by the construction and opening of the Newcastle & Berwick Railway. The 1st Edition of the Ordnance maps shows that by the date of the survey in the 1850s the lower part of the line, between the main line railway and the Jetty, had been dismantled, along with the 'machine house' at Cliff Rest which had contained the machinery and engine for working wagons on the gradient down to Spittal. The outlet for the coal became the newly-built connection between the upper part of the Scremerston Railway and sidings constructed to the west of the Newcastle to Berwick main line. The tunnel which had formerly led the coal railway under the Newcastle and Berwick line was abandoned. By this time the line to the colliery was certainly a 'railway' not a 'plateway'.

6 – The Scremerston Railway

The Greenwich Colliery continued in operation, in the hands of the Scremerston and Shoreswood Colliery Company, until its closure at the end of the 1880s. It was under this company that the Scremerston Railway had become linked to the main line railway system. There were distinct advantages arising from this. Larger, 'main-line-type' wagons could be taken to the colliery and loaded directly before return to the main railway system for distribution. Greater speed of movement and shortened delivery times could be expected. However, some strengthening of the colliery rails would have been inevitable together with some mechanization at the colliery.

The Greenwich Colliery had several sidings for wagons awaiting loading. From the colliery the single line Scremerston Railway headed almost due north up a gradient of about 1 in 55. It reached its summit close to the level crossing by the Scremerston village chapel. From here it descended at a gentler gradient until it passed Restoration Cottages and arrived adjacent to the site of the former Restoration Pit. Here it turned towards the north-east and, shortly afterwards, reached another level crossing over the road to Borewell and Cocklawburn. Continuing in a straight line, almost on the level, for another 100 yards it made a sharp curve to bring it onto a north-south alignment. Here the downwards gradient began in earnest, at about 1 in 25, towards the North Eastern Railway's Newcastle to Berwick main line. The track on the gradient was straight and to facilitate this the line towards the top of the incline was built on an embankment rising to 10 metres in height in places. Lower down it entered a shallow cutting before becoming double tracked, curving to the left to terminate in the loop of the exchange sidings adjacent to the main line. Here the loaded coal wagons were

Restoration Cottages, Scremerston, which pre-dated Deputy Row, were built for the miners at Scremerston's Restoration Pit. They are located adjacent to the former colliery site just a few hundred yards from the head of the Scremerston incline. *Author*

The cottages, known as Deputy Row, were built for the miners and other workers associated with Scremerston Pit. They survive today at the side of the former A1 road on the outskirts of Scremerston village. *Author*

handed over to the NER and 'empties' were left ready for return to the colliery. At first the 'old alignment' towards Spittal remained, passing under the main line by means of a short tunnel or underbridge. Later this feature was removed.

Initially haulage of wagons on the gradient was by means of an engine house and winch located at the top of the incline. It seems likely that only after the demise of the Greenwich Pit and the opening of the 'New Winning Pit' (later 'Scremerston Colliery') that locomotives may have been employed though a comment by one of the colliery Directors may hint otherwise (see later).

One sad event was reported in the local newspapers in March 1861 when an orphaned boy, joyriding on a wagon on the Scremerston Colliery line, was run over and killed.

In the late 1870s the Greenwich Pit closed and the new pit was sunk, to the Cooper Eye seam, by the Scremerston & Shoreswood Colliery Co. In 1893 the company became the Scremerston Coal Co., a further name change taking place in 1905 when it became the Scremerston Coal Co. Ltd. One of the Directors of these companies, J.E. Carr, mentioned above, made a very interesting statement in an edition of the *Berwick Advertiser* in 1931. When referring, presumably, to the end of the Greenwich Pit, he said: 'In the final two decades of the life of Scremerston Colliery the coal was hauled from the pithead by the engine 'Puffing Billy' down the old line to the Newcastle to Berwick Railway.' Was his memory at fault or was there, indeed, an 'old-type' steam locomotive in use on the colliery line and incline at this time? Appearing to support Carr's statement there is an engraving by J. Gellatly of Edinburgh, entitled 'The Shipping Place of the Greenwich Hospital Coals' (used on the company's letter heading) which depicts the coal jetty at Spittal with a three-masted sailing vessel at anchor (see page 52). There is no doubt about the identity of the location as the Old Berwick bridge appears in the background on the right-hand side of the engraving. In the centre are six coal-filled tubs standing on the jetty with what appears to be a seventh being lifted, or tipped, into the hold of the vessel. On the left-hand side of the picture is depicted a train of seven coal wagons being hauled by a steam locomotive. The view of the locomotive is drawn from the rear and there is no detail of the locomotive apart from its huge chimney, indicating that it is certainly of an 'early' type. It would seem that Carr may have been correct in his reference to locomotive haulage even if the locomotive was not the original *Puffing Billy*!

The new pit was located to the west of the Great North Road (NU004497). The line from Restoration Cottages to the Greenwich Pit was lifted and a line laid to the new one. It left the former alignment at the site of the old Restoration Pit and curved towards the west, rising gently, before a level crossing of the Great North Road which was to survive until the final abandonment of Scremerston Colliery in September 1944. Immediately after the crossing the line curved towards the north west and then north, passing to the west of Deputy Row Cottages, before entering the colliery premises.

The Scremerston Coal Co. Ltd is known to have operated two steam locomotives in addition to the horses that have appeared in photographs of the colliery. (The colliery possessed its own smithy.) The records of the Industrial Locomotive Society and the Industrial Railway Society identify the first locomotive as an Andrew Barclay-built 0-4-0 saddle tank, with outside cylinders, Works No. 251 of 1882. This had arrived from the Broxburn Oil Co. Ltd of West Lothian in Scotland, sometime after August 1912. The second locomotive was a Manning, Wardle 0-6-0 saddle tank, with inside cylinders, Works No. 1204 of 1890, which arrived from the contractors J. Parkinson & Son. It arrived some time after February 1917 and possibly carried the name *Thornhill*. These two locomotives shared the traffic until the mid-1930s. The subsequent fate of neither is known; they may have been sold for further use elsewhere, or in view of their age, scrapped.

It was in December 1935 that Scremerston Colliery was purchased by C.A. Nelson, the Chairman of Hartley Main Collieries Ltd, and a new company, Scremerston Main Collieries Ltd, was formed under the Chairmanship of H. K. Newcombe. Shortly after this a locomotive was transferred from the Hartley Main colliery system near to Cramlington in the south of the county. It still carried its Hartley Main number, 'No. 13', whilst working at Scremerston. This locomotive was an outside-cylindered 0-4-0 saddle tank built by Robert Stephenson & Co. with Works No. 2841 of 1896. This locomotive had worked since new for the Cramlington Coal Co. until 16th May, 1929 when this company was absorbed by Hartley Main. It worked at Scremerston until the colliery closure in 1944.

After the colliery closed an auction of the plant at Scremerston was conducted. This took place on 24th October, 1944. The sale catalogue included an old saddle tank locomotive with 14 in. by 18 in. cylinders, presumably No. 2841. It left Scremerston following this, its destination unknown. Fortunately one 1930s picture of this locomotive working at Scremerston has been traced. In the photograph it still carries its Hartley Main livery and number.

The colliery had several sidings for storage of wagons and tracks which passed beneath screens where the wagons were loaded. One line is shown on Ordnance Survey maps as entering one of the buildings which may thus have been a locomotive shed. In view of the 1 in 25 gradient, and especially on wet days, it was necessary to pin down the brakes on loaded wagons as the 'fulls' were being taken down to the exchange sidings!

In the 1890s the colliery employed around 150 men. This total rose to a maximum of 275 by 1921 but after this date the number slowly but steadily declined until just over a hundred were employed before the 1944 closure. In 1940 coal production was 100,000 tons. Many men transferred to the newly-opened Blackhill Colliery (NT983477) a few miles away, also operated by the Hartley Main Co.

7 – The Unthank Waggonway

The Unthank Waggonway was an early 19th century line which linked Unthank Colliery with Tweedmouth. It was variously described in documents as a waggonway, wagonway, railway, tramway or tramroad! The colliery, with several others including Murton and Billy Law collieries, was located on Unthank Moor, some 3¾ miles to the south-west of Berwick. Some of the coal from these pits was for landsale (either at the colliery or at Tweedmouth), some was used at the local limekilns, whilst the remainder was exported from the port of Tweedmouth on the south bank of the Tweed.

The earliest discovered written record of the colliery is a lease to a certain Mr Robson of Wallington in 1776; some secondary sources have previously quoted 1766. Prior to this, small quantities of landsale coal had been obtained from the area, some pits having been operational as early as 1744.

Early in the 18th century Unthank was a portion of the estate of the Orde family. Various collieries were located elsewhere on the Orde Estate, such as those at East and Middle Orde. Many of these were shallow pits, Unthank being regarded as the deepest at 48 fathoms (288 ft) where it tapped the Fawcett seam; it was provided with a couple of engines for pumping and lifting. The family also owned a staithe at Tweedmouth which was used for the export of some coal from the port.

In 1774 the Unthank portion of the estate, by now owned by Sir Walter Blackett, passed into the hands of John Selby of Beal. On 1st January, 1777 Selby leased Unthank Colliery to Messrs Fenwick Stow, Elias Boreham and George Douglas for a term of 21 years at a rent of £200 per year.

In 1809 Selby was still the owner and his colliery tenant was a John Jackson (the younger) who employed 15 hewers at the pit. By 1811 Jackson was declared bankrupt.

In early 1824 the colliery was described as closed but later that year Selby leased the colliery (on a seven year lease) to a local man, John Sibbitt(s), who lifted some coal and sent it by cart to Budle for onward passage by sea. This was not an efficient way of distributing coal, bearing in mind the poor state of the roads between Unthank and Budle. Therefore, within a couple of years Selby made a financial investment in the form of a loan of £3,000 for the construction of the waggonway or railway which was to create an upturn the fortunes of the colliery. The advertisement shown below was placed in the *Berwick Advertiser* regarding the construction of the line (Greenses House and hamlet was located about a mile to the south-east of the colliery).

The lessee, John Sibbits [sic], wrote to Selby in these terms: 'I can assure you that when the Railway is completed all persons will be much indebted. John Sibbits (Berwick) 26.8.1826.'

RAILWAY
FROM
UNTHANK COLLIERY TO TWEEDMOUTH.

ESTIMATES will be received by Mr. BALMER, Ancroft Greenses, on WEDNESDAY the 6th September next, at Three o'Clock, P. M. for Cutting and Mounding sundry parts of the intended Railway. Particulars are inserted in the Handbills, which may be had by applying at Tweedmouth Low Gate.

Greenses, *August* 24th, 1826.

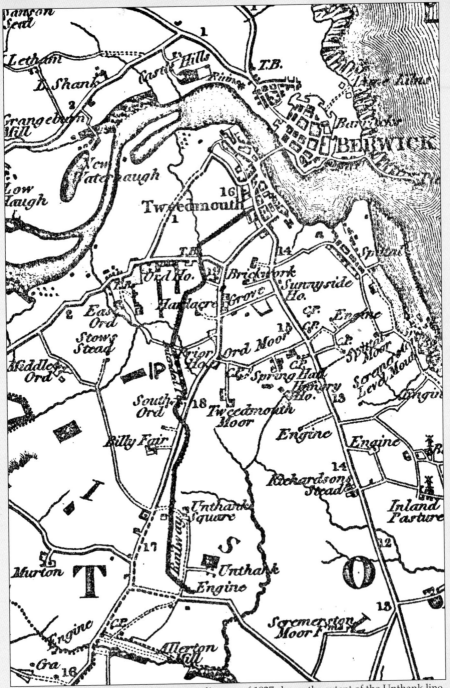

An enlargement of a portion of Greenwood's map of 1827 shows the extent of the Unthank line, marked as a 'railway', linking the collieries with Tweedmouth. The inclined plane at South Ord was clearly incomplete at the time of Greenwood's survey as it is marked 'Intended'.

Berwick-upon-Tweed Record Office

The building of the waggonway is surprisingly well-documented, largely as a result of the local newspaper carrying a detailed account. In September 1826 it stated '… the parties contracted for the cutting of the Railway are getting on with far more expedition than ever …' The contract for laying the line had been placed with Sheridan Dunn of Durham after John Longstaff of Durham had performed the levelling. Henry Menzies had been appointed for the hauling of ballast to the line and James Brown was appointed to lay the ballast on the alignment of the railway. John Dobs & Co. were charged with '… winning of stone for the railway …' Albert Grigson was responsible for the sawing of all timber used.

The line was laid with 'malleable iron, flat [bottomed?] rails' in 9 ft, 12 ft and 15 ft lengths. The first of these arrived in the month of September 1826. A total of 1,118 'bars' of rail was used on the line. The rail weighed 17 lb. per yard. It was laid in chairs with either single or double holes for the fixing spikes. The bill for the rails and chairs was for the sum of £1,889 11s. 1d. A discount on the cost of the rails would be obtained if the bill was paid within three months of delivery. In all 1,731 ft of wood was used for 'laying the way' presumably a reference to the sleepers. The line was provided with wooden gates and posts where it crossed public roads and paths. There were 17 or 18 men generally at work on the line and they were paid the sum of 1s. 6d. per day. One unfortunate accident occurred during the construction of the line. This occurred on 16th June, 1827 when Andrew Porteous, a labourer, was crushed to death by a caving-in which occurred whilst he was digging on the line.

The bill for the blacksmith's work amounted to £18 7s. 8d. In September 1827 Selby entered into a Contract with Michael Longridge for the supply of iron rails from the Bedlington Iron Co. Also, in December 1827, a letter from a Mr Russell of Alnwick (it is not known what his role was) referred to the delivery of some 'iron railways plates and metal chairs' for the line. These were possibly spares or replacements. The term 'plates' appears to be at odds with the earlier description of the iron rails. Perhaps the term was being used in a different context.

An undated letter, simply addressed to 'Sir' but possibly referring to Selby, the lessor, referred to the inclined plane on the line and the placing of two wagons at its head: 'a wonderful exhibition'! On 6th November, 1827 the local newspaper reported that: 'The Railway is now completed and it is ascertained beyond a doubt it will answer an excellent purpose as it will cause the Colliery to compete in vend with any Colliery in the neighbourhood.'

The horse-drawn loaded coal wagons left the sidings at Unthank Colliery and headed north, passing just to the west of the houses of Unthank Square, still present today. Parts of the fields in this vicinity still show evidence of the small embankments which were constructed to even out the gradient of the line and to raise it above the somewhat boggy fields. The line curved eastwards slightly to run parallel to the Berwick to Duddo road, until it passed about 100 yards to the east of the old Billy Law Colliery (located on the west side of the same road). The Unthank line then curved to the left, crossed the road on the level and then headed almost due north towards the summit of the line which was reached at Ord. It then descended with embankments being used, once again, to even out the gradients. (Some evidence of this part of the line survived into the 1960s though the building of the Berwick by-pass resulted in most disappearing.) The line continued to head

Some of the Unthank Wagonway crossed land which became boggy in winter. For this reason, and to even out gradients, part of the line was constructed upon shallow embankments including this part crossing a field close to Unthank Square.   *Author*

The building of the railway between Newcastle and Berwick necessitated the building of a large embankment leading to the Royal Border bridge over the River Tweed. A pair of tunnels leading through the embankment was built to allow the Unthank line to maintain its access to Tweedmouth. However, they were barely used as the Unthank line closed shortly afterwards.   *Author*

approximately north until it curved sharply eastwards running between the houses towards its terminus at the coal yard in Tweedmouth, next to the Great North Road. The construction of the main line railway through Tweedmouth towards Berwick necessitated the inclusion of a pair of tunnels in the embankment to accommodate the wagons of the Unthank line passing beneath. One 1850s map, however, shows the Unthank line as terminating to the west of the tunnels. These tunnels survive today, though linking areas of private land.

The line then settled down to perform the function for which it was built, namely facilitating the transport of coal from Unthank to the port of Tweedmouth. Reports exist of some coals being 'exported' to the ports of Eyemouth and Alnmouth and some being transported by carts the additional quarter of a mile between Tweedmouth and Berwick. The number of pitmen at this time is not recorded but 12 ponies were employed underground. The men lived in small houses at nearby Murton Square and in other isolated dwellings. A cooper was employed for making the wooden tubs used for moving coal. A list described as 'Labourers and other persons employed above ground on the Railway and Depots of Berwick and Tweedmouth, and Waggonmen' refers to three 'waggonwaywrights', four men working in the coalyard at Tweedmouth and two men in the Berwick depot. It also refers to a 'Keeper of waggonway horses'. A wayleave rent was paid for each wagon of coal to pass along the line from the colliery to Tweedmouth.

After the line was completed, Sibbitt negotiated a new lease; this was dated 2nd September, 1828, then subsequently a further one dated 12th May, 1830. He also took out a lease on the nearby Murton Colliery just ½ mile away. He proposed a linking railway from there to Unthank but it is not known if this materialized. Certainly a 'cartroad' was laid in 1831 from this colliery to nearby limekilns so it would seem that these did not receive a waggonway link. The same year the pitmen, seeing the success of the colliery, applied for a wage increase.

A document dated 1832 gives a good indication of the success of the colliery and waggonway at this time. There was a vend of 30,000 tons annually (including both landsale coal and that exported via Tweedmouth) with some 30,000 bolls (6,222 cu. yds) being used at the local limekilns. Further references are made to the possibility of lime from the local kilns being moved along the line but it is not known whether this ever supplemented the coal traffic. In May 1832 it was expected that Sibbit would repay the loan of £3,000 to Selby. Sibbitt (using the solicitors James Russell of Narrowgate, Alnwick) attempted to sub-let the colliery and waggonway to a certain Mr W. Smith. Sibbitt would repay to Selby the £3,000, the interest owed and any costs, together with any charges for damages caused by 'the railroad'. It is not known if this sub-let went ahead because the pitmen once again started to cause trouble over the level of their wages!

An advertisement appeared in the local newspaper dated 8th July, 1842 after the death of Sibbitt some time earlier:

UNTHANK COLLIERY
Near Berwick on Tweed
To be sold by proposal for the Residue of the Term of the Present Lease, Unthank Colliery with houses, machinery, railway and materials and appurtenances.

The documentation referred to the Colliery, with a face of 600 yards, as producing the best coal in the district! It stated that, '... the railroad [sic] from the Colliery to a depot at Tweedmouth, a short distance from Berwick Quay, affords, in conjunction with other local appurtenances, decided facilities for Coasting and Foreign trade in coal'. It also referred to '... a great and unfailing trade for land coal (independent of the need for the railway)'. The advertisement was signed by Thomas Murray, the colliery Manager.

George Carr, with interests at other local collieries such as Shoreswood, took over the lease, though in 1845 he experienced difficulties with his workforce who pursued legal means regarding their perceived inadequate remuneration. Plans drawn up at this time to link the Colliery (and that at Shoreswood) with the Berwick to Kelso railway did not materialize.

James Raine's book, *The History and Antiquities of North Durham*, published in 1852, referred to the railway as '...laid to Tweedmouth, or Spittal, by means of which Mr Selby is enabled to convey his coals to the sea'. However, in May 1851 Selby had sold his estate to Robert Crossman (who had homes in both London and Berwick). The Board of Health Map of 1852 showed the Unthank line running beneath the main line of the York, Berwick & Newcastle Railway yet the line did not appear on the 'Plan of Berwick, Tweedmouth and Spittal', dated the same year. The first Ordnance Survey map, surveyed in the mid-1850s showed that the line had been lifted and its former trackbed was shown only intermittently. Parts were labelled 'Old Tramway'. No tunnel was indicated under the Berwick & Kelso Railway (actually Tweedmouth to Kelso) and it is possible that the Unthank line had ceased to function by the time this was built in 1849. The fate of the lifted rails is not known; searches of the local field boundaries have failed to reveal any lengths in use as fenceposts, as has happened elsewhere.

The *Newcastle Weekly Chronicle* of 29th November, 1873 referred to '... the deserted pit heaps of Unthank...'. By that time the new pit at Billy Law, to the east of the Berwick to Duddo road and worked by Johnson and Carr, had assumed the role of the local landsale colliery (producing, for example, between 40 and 50 tons per day in 1873).

However, in 1886 Charles Selby Bigge leased the Unthank Colliery to a consortium including Thomas Jackson, John Carr, C.H. Carr and George Dryden Carr. This lease referred to the colliery and *underground* waggonways but not to the long-lifted railway. This colliery took over from Billy Law as the local landsale colliery. It was worked with some success: in 1897 over 7,900 tons of coal were won and the maximum of 11,778 tons was lifted in 1901. However, after this peak, coal production here declined and in 1905 work was suspended at the pit. By this time it was owned by the Scremerston Coal Co. The men were transferred to the nearby Allerdean and Scremerston pits.

8 – The Shoreswood Colliery Tramway

The Scremerston coal seams extend westwards and several bell pits and collieries were opened on Ancroft Moor in the early 19th century. Surviving records indicate that pits were operating at Shoreswood in 1816, 1819, January 1825, and 1828. In

1816, for example, the estimated yearly value of the coal produced was £250. This coal was landsale coal for local domestic use. (In 1825 three of the pit boys from Shoreswood were sent for trial for killing a pony with great barbarity!)

Shoreswood Colliery (NT957461) is recorded alternatively as 'Shaws Wood Colliery', and, more recently as 'Shoresdean Colliery'. It was worked with varying degrees of success and was often beset with problems. It was located at Shoresdean to the west of the Berwick to Wooler road (now the B6354), some 5 miles south-west of Berwick and ½ mile to the north-west of Ancroft Northmoor. The road linking the Berwick road with Norham ran some 600 yards to the north of the colliery site, passing Shoreswood Hall. At least two shafts were sunk at the site. There were three workable coal seams here: the main coal seam, known locally as the 'Bulman seam' (about 22 fathoms (132 ft) down and up to 7 ft 7 in. thick, though with some chalk and grey stone), the small '¾ Eye seam', and the 'Cooper (or Cupar) Eye seam' (41 fathoms (246 ft) down and 3 ft 3 in. thick but of good quality coal).

By November 1836 the colliery was held under lease (together with the nearby Thornton Pit) from the Dean and Chapter of Durham and the Craster family of Craster House. The tithe map of the area, dated 1839, but with an accompanying tithe award dated 7th February, 1845, indicates two collieries with a line of tramway from one of them to the nearby Ancroft to Norham road. The details of the lease refer to the colliery as having a depth from the bottom of the pit to the 'scaffold' of 27 fathoms (162 ft). The 'main engine' for the pit was a beam engine, described as being single-powered with a 4 lb. or 5 lb. pressure. It powered 12 in. pumps which worked for 12 hours per day on each day of the week, removing much water. The pit had a 200 yards-long coalface, employed 36 hewers (earning 18s. per week) and nine horses were used.

A few years later the colliery is described as '…belonging to John Sibbitt who works her'. In reality Sibbitt probably leased the colliery as he had leased Unthank and other collieries to the north. He worked, principally, the Cooper Eye seam.

Fresh borings were made by Messrs Carr & Co. in 1843 and a new shaft was sunk, revealing the Bulman seam and the Cooper Eye seam; the events were accompanied by much optimism. A 'Shoreswood Colliery Office' was opened in Berwick-upon-Tweed. This office issued, in February 1849, an invitation to 'Contractors and others' to tender for the building of the 'Shoreswood Branch' to join the about-to-be-completed Kelso Railway at Velvet Hall. Plans for the proposed line could be inspected at the Colliery Office. Unfortunately these plans have not survived. The colliery owners did not bind themselves to accept the lowest offer! It is not known how many tenders were received by the closing date of Saturday 10th March. Naught came of this scheme and a small tramway represented the only line of rails to serve the colliery.

The narrow gauge tramway (sometimes recorded as a waggonway) linked the pithead with the Ancroft to Norham road at a site known as 'Peterhead' adjacent to the present Shoresdean crossroads. The line was built as the surroundings of the pit could become marshy and movement by cart would have been difficult. Its construction was straightforward as no substantial earthworks were involved and the gradients were slight. Some 200 tons of coal were moved along the line each day. At Peterhead was a landsale site where, according to one record, there would be '… farm carts and drivers clamouring for coal…' In winter approximately 400 to 500 carts would arrive each day for loading. Whilst some of these were local, others came from Scotland. Some of the Scottish hauliers took the coal for long distances. It is recorded that many overnighted with their loads at an establishment called 'The Old Wagon', or 'The Wagonway Inn' at Kelso. The horses working the tramway would have been kept busy.

The parish, by 1860, had a population of between 400 and 500, chiefly miners and their dependants. Many lived close to the colliery in one-roomed houses at 'The Folly'. Others lived in more widely-scattered houses. The spare-time hobbies of the miners were described as gambling, dog fancying and rabbit coursing!

The ownership of the colliery and its various lessees is somewhat confusing. In 1855 written evidence suggests that a certain George Wood was both the farmer and the coal proprietor at Shoreswood. However, *Whellan's Directory* of the same year describes the land as being owned by Thomas Wood Craster of Craster House, but with Messrs Carr & Co. as the colliery proprietors. *Kelly's Directory* of 1858 described the 'owners' as Robert Johnson & Co.! However, in 1862 a new document was drawn up by Messrs Thorp & Dickson, solicitors, of Alnwick, for the lease of the land from the trustees of the late Lord Crewe. This contains some useful details of the colliery and the tramway. The lease, to last for 21 years, specified a rent of £50 per annum for leading coal from the shafts plus '…640 tens of coals at 2/6d per ten…' (a 'ten' is specified as a chaldron holding 53 cwt of coal). Just one line of railway was permitted, plus sidings, the route of which could not be changed. The line was to transport coal or coke from the colliery site and to bring any iron or timber for use at the colliery. The land for the tramway was not to exceed 14 yards in width and it was to be both maintained with railings and gated. There should be proper culverts and drains and crossing places for roads or footpaths. Such crossings should be supplied with attendants. Coals from other pits in the area would not be allowed to be moved along the line. In addition any manure deposited on the tramway was to belong to the tenants of the ground. They were granted the liberty to move such manure along the line using wagons with suitable wheels! The first edition of the Ordnance Maps, surveyed at about this time, indicates the line of this tramway from the colliery which is shown to have two shafts, an engine house and smithy. The lease appears to have been take up by Messrs Johnson & Carr, who became the proprietors, adding Shoreswood to their other industrial local interests.

The *Berwick Advertiser* of 20th July, 1866 contained a letter, written to the Editor from London by a person who signed himself 'Flat Justice'. The author of the letter, who claimed that Berwick was his 'native place', complained about '… a very serious encroachment on public right in the Parish of Norham…'. Apparently for some years he had been riding on horseback from Berwickshire, over the Union Bridge, then via Norham, Etal, Horncliffe, Thornton, Shoreswood, Felkington and Duddo. For some two or three years he had found that part of his route, namely that between Thornton and Shoreswood, had been 'stopped to the public'. He added,

A tramway, constructed I understand by the Shoreswood Colliery Company for conveying their coal from the pit to the bottom of the lane, actually occupies part of the highway itself for a distance of between three and four hundred yards, thus completely blocking up the road to riders and also horses in carts; for who, on horseback would dare to meet a train of these tubs rolling over the hill on this tramway at the risk of breaking his neck.

He added that the diversion to escape 'this intolerable nuisance' involved an additional 1½ miles of travel over an inferior road. He called on the 'Waywardens' and local gentlemen to ensure that the route was kept clear, particularly as the road led to the new Velvet Hall station on the NER's Kelso branch. He expressed his hope that 'the public grievance' could be reduced.

The colliery continued to produce coal for another 20 years or so, though in 1873 the *Newcastle Weekly Chronicle* declared that the colliery's best coal winning days were long past. (Its first recorded fatality had occurred in 1873 when one of the hewers, Thomas Ingres, was killed by a fall of stone.) However, the 1881 census indicated that there were still over 40 employed at the colliery, including 27 coalminers, three putters, two banksmen, two weighmen, two engine drivers, three engine kippers and a couple of blacksmiths.

By 1894 the colliery was disused after having spent the last years of its life performing the duty of a pumping shaft for the nearby Felkington Colliery. The abandonment plan indicated that the final coal had been removed from the Cooper Eye seam. Contractors moved in to break up some of the plant and salvage useful materials. The Ordnance map of the same year indicates that the tramway had also been lifted after a working life of about 50 years. A second fatal accident was to occur at the colliery when one of the contractor's men, employed to break up some old metal with dynamite, fell from the engine bed to his death.

A survey of the remains at the site performed in August 1973 identified the remains of the colliery buildings, the engine house, the mine pumping house, the winding house and the blacksmith's hearth. These have now largely disappeared. The line of the tramway survives, partly as an unmarked footpath and partly as the tarmac road leading to the hamlet of Shoresdean. No remains exist at the landsale depot at 'Peterhead' crossroads.

The Shoreswood Colliery Tramway followed the fence in the centre of this 2011 picture linking the pit with a coal depot, known as 'Peterhead', on the north side of the Ancroft to Norham Road. A bus shelter now occupies the depot's location. Norham station was closed in the 1960s! Shoreswood Hall and farm form the backdrop.   *Author*

9 – The Allerdean Drift Railway

Blackhill Colliery was sunk in 1942 to replace the colliery at Scremerston which was closing. Before nationalization it had two owners: John Watson & Co. (of Scotland) and Young Ltd. It had two short coal faces of just 30 yards and 60 yards in length. This colliery, which had severe water problems, was never rail-connected, all coal being taken away by road for the local use. Despite a campaign by the local communities, well reported in the local press, the National Coal Board closed the mine on 20th February, 1959.

Some of the redundant Blackhill miners, faced with little prospect of alternative employment, made an arrangement with the Elsdon Colliery Co. Ltd (of Otterburn in Redesdale) to reopen the old Allerdean Drift (NT969465), located not far from the site of the closed Blackhill pit. Just over 30 men were employed at the pit, some 24 of these working below ground.

The drift was approached via a gate leading into the hillside. A single line of narrow gauge railway was laid from the surface down an incline to the pit face. This incline was cable-worked and loaded wagons were hauled to the surface by a fixed diesel engine. The steel cable ran over rollers which were fixed to the sleepers between the rails. A short trap-siding, to prevent runaway vehicles descending the steep gradient into the shaft, was located just outside the pit gate. This line was also used to house spare wagons.

This pit operated for several years, selling its coal to local merchants supplying household coal or to firms to feed local boilers, until a tragedy in the mid-1960s caused its closure. The entrance to the shaft collapsed and the face was lost. Unfortunately one man was killed in the accident.

The railway at Allerdean Drift consisted of a cable-worked incline leading from the mine to the surface. Here a loaded tub approaches the surface. The points here were 'sprung' so that a runaway wagon would be diverted to the spur on the right to prevent it descending uncontrollably into the mine.   *Jack Parsons*

Chapter Five

The Colliery Railways of the Amble Area

The industrial railways of the Amble area were built for two purposes: firstly to link the local collieries with an outlet to the sea at the mouth of the River Coquet, and secondly for the construction, subsequent improvement and operation of the facilities at what was formerly called Warkworth Harbour. The earliest lines were those built in the late 1830s. The first linked the newly-sunk Radcliffe Colliery with a small loading point or staithe on the south bank of the Coquet. Shortly afterwards a quarry line was constructed which was associated with the building of the harbour. Later the Amble brickworks was constructed adjacent to the harbour. This works, which received its fireclay and coal from Radcliffe until the 1890s, had its own sidings and internal narrow gauge lines. The original Radcliffe line was later extended and linked to Broomhill Colliery (originally Newburgh Colliery) in 1893. (This colliery and its railways are located outside the Alnwick District and therefore beyond the scope of this book.) Finally a branch from the Radcliffe line provided an outlet for Hauxley Colliery opened in 1926. The branch line between Amble and the East Coast main line at Chevington (linked with Broomhill Colliery and others) is also outside the scope of this work. Other isolated lines, such as that on the Amble North Pier and the craneway on the South Pier, were derivatives of some of the earlier lines.

75

10 – The Radcliffe Colliery Wagonway and later railways towards Newburgh and Broomhill Collieries

A newspaper reference to a Grant by Charter for 'coal mynes in Amble' is one of the earliest written references to the coal industry in the area. In 1772 the *Newcastle Courant* referred to '...natural features at the mouth of the Coquet being admirably suited and adapted for a harbour ... with a fine seam of coal abounding in the adjoining ground'.

At this time the Amble Estate belonged to the Earl of Newburgh, the land to the north of the River Coquet being referred to as the 'Countess of Newburgh Links'. The population of the area in 1831 was just 247 and it was a fairly desolate spot. Various sources indicate that commercial coal extraction in the area commenced on a small scale in 1834 or 1835. However, it was not until January 1837, when a certain Mr Kingscote commenced the sinking of a pit on Clarke's South Moor constructing associated buildings and a pond, that coal mining here took place on an industrial scale. Kingscote is believed to have come from Bedlington and had previously speculated at Sleekburn Colliery. Kingscote's pit was to become known as the Radcliffe Colliery, situated at NU270027 on present OS maps. It may be that mining actually commenced slightly before the drawing up of the lease as various records refer to the sinking of the 'First Pit' in 1836.

Kingscote owned the colliery buildings and plant which were constructed on Newburgh land, though later additional land was obtained from the Board of Trade Commissioners. The lease for working the coal was drawn up on 7th January, 1837 (later sources say it took effect from 15th October, 1837) between Ann, Dowager Countess of Newburgh, and a consortium including Messrs Philip Henry Howard, Robert Ladbroke and Thomas Brown. The last two gentlemen were described as 'trustees' in the agreement, presumably trustees of the late Earl's interests. The surname of the Earl and Countess was Radclyffe. The lease was for 45 years, though they relinquished it in the 1840s; the colliery was subsequently operated by the harbour company. The site of the proposed colliery and the alignment of the associated wagonway were probably surveyed in 1836 after an advertisement had been placed for an enginewright to inspect the site for the location of machinery and a 'railroad'.

From the new pit at Clarke's South Moor Field the Radcliffe wagonway (or railroad) headed northwards for some 1¼ miles crossing the land of Messrs James Dand, John Wellwood and T. George Smith to whom wayleave payments were made. Smith also received the sum of £150 for 'damages' after various court cases. The line was nearly straight and was well constructed with a drainage ditch on either side of the trackbed. It was constructed on land which virtually eliminated gradients, the steepest on the line being 1 in 426. The construction made use of 'stone, wood and rails'. It terminated at the side of the River Coquet to the east of a small stream known as the 'Gut'. Here a small staithe was constructed, known as 'Smith's Staithe'. The first coals were moved along the line on 3rd October, 1837. A further survey was conducted on 5th April, 1838, though for what purpose is not known. Perhaps it was to verify that the terms in the agreement had been met. Landsale coal was available from 17th

October, 1838. Some of the first colliers had 'migrated' from the pits at Shilbottle to find better employment at Radcliffe.

At this time the pit had reached a depth of '11 fathoms' (66 ft) and a small seam, just two feet thick, could be tapped. Apparently wagons for use on the line were stored at the river end and worked to the colliery when needed. Some riverside sidings were provided for this purpose. At this time there was little at Amble apart from the wagonway and the staithe which reached from high water mark to low water mark. A second staithe was constructed shortly after, though, at this time only vessels of very low draught could use the port.

It was in 1837 that the Warkworth Harbour Commissioners obtained an Act of Parliament to build a proper harbour at what is now Amble. A certain John Straker had inspected the colliery and staithes and reported that Amble Harbour was '… a bad one as the winds from the north-east will be very severe upon the shipping for want of shelter'. (Straker also reported that some water was entering the Pit. Later a 150 hp condensing engine would be used to keep the pit dry.) A harbour company was formed with the trustees of the Earl of Newburgh, the lessees of the colliery and the Duke of Northumberland all being represented. Four plans for the layout of the harbour were submitted, that of well-known engineer and surveyor John Rennie being accepted. It involved the construction of a 2,300 ft-long northern breakwater and a 600 ft southern breakwater with an entrance some 250 ft in width. This would, it was stated, protect the mouth of the river and some 14 ft of water would be maintained at the bar at low tide. His Plan, dated 31st March, 1838, showed that the Coquet was to be narrowed considerably, necessitating an extension of the Radcliffe line by several hundred yards to the north and the construction of a new staithe. The narrowing was to increase the velocity of the water flowing downstream and thus hopefully to eliminate the deposition of sand and silt in the port. Later plans show that Rennie's original scheme was to undergo some modification. The contractors appointed were Messrs James & John Welch and five years were allowed for them to complete the work. However, they were replaced by Messrs Sandersons in the early 1840s as the work had not progressed satisfactorily.

The contractors built a house, known as Cliff House, near Pan Point to the east of the staithes; this later housed a small Chapel for Roman Catholic workers and also a 'tommy shop' where the workmen could exchange the tokens, with which they were paid, for foods and other goods. It is said that '…crowds of workmen' invaded the area to find work on the harbour project!

A quarry beneath Pan Point (at Pan Haven Rocks) was opened to provide sandstone for the breakwaters (and later also for parts of the developing town). This quarry was just inland from the sea cliffs on land belonging to George Smith. Evidence from Sopwith & Scott's July 1840 'Plan of the Township of Amble' (*see page 79*) suggests that Pan Rocks themselves may have provided some stone until the quarry was opened. According to the plan, a small railway was laid from three sidings at Pan Rocks and it followed the line of the high water mark alongside the River Coquet. This line was to facilitate the movement of stone for the construction of the North Breakwater (described on Sopwith & Scott's plan as 'now forming'). However, reaching this site necessitated the

The contractors constructing Warkworth Harbour built Cliff House, near to Pan Point. It was used to house a Roman Catholic chapel and also a 'tommy shop' where the workmen could exchange tokens for goods and food. The quarry beneath the house, in the foreground, was used to provide sandstone for the building of the harbour piers. *Author*

The offices of the Warkworth Harbour Commissioners are still in daily use at Harbour Road in Amble. The internal walls of the offices are adorned with historic pictures of the harbour in its heyday when its staithes and moorings were busy with visiting vessels. *Inset:* This highly-polished, and difficult to photograph, plaque, dating from the mid-19th century, remains attached to the wall of the offices at Amble adjacent to the main entrance door. *(Both) Author*

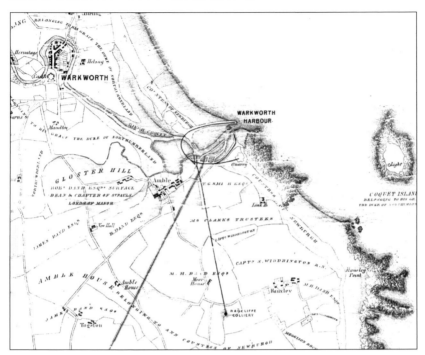

Sopwith & Scott's plan shows Warkworth Harbour in the 1840s and the railway to bring rock from the quarry near to Pan Rocks for the building of the North Pier. The tramway linking Radcliffe Colliery with the harbour and the new branch (then under construction) linking Amble with the Newcastle & Berwick Railway are also shown.

Northumberland Record Office

construction of a temporary railway crossing of the Coquet. Accordingly a viaduct on timber piles was built, crossing over the river at 'The Braid', the name given to a small, low-lying muddy region in the river. Later the line was moved to start from the quarry being developed inland from Pan Rocks.

A letter signed by a certain Nicholas Wood and dated 29th July, 1840, takes the form of a report which contains the following:

> To accomplish the formation of the North Pier of the Harbour, a timber platform has been erected across the river and a railway laid thereon and extending also from the quarries on the south side of the river to the pier and a locomotive engine employed in carrying stones for the formation thereof. The piling has been put in for a considerable distance and the timber platform and the railway placed thereon. Since the erection of the platform and railway a considerable quantity of stones has been deposited and the contractor appears to me to be using every practical exertion in quarrying and depositing the stones.

Radcliffe Colliery letterheading.   *Durham Record Office*

By 1841, however, the contractors were in some difficulty and the colliery company applied for £36,000 for the completion of the harbour works. By 8th October, 1841 the North Pier was within 17 ft of the terminal buoy and only two to three months would be needed for the piling, with the rest of the stone work planned for completion by the end of the year. The completion of the shorter South Pier (not started at the time of Sopwith's plan) was planned for the same time. However, the local sandstone proved to be too soft for its purpose and after much erosion it was replaced by Scottish granite. Altogether some £175,000 was spent on the completion of the works.

On the north side of the river a small wooden hut or shed was constructed over the rail line. This housed the small steam locomotive, referred to, in sources dating from the 1860s, as '...a small puffing billy, one of the first of its kind '. The identity of this locomotive has not been confirmed though Industrial Railway Society records indicate that a small Robert Stephenson-built 0-4-0 outside cylinder saddle tank locomotive worked on the Radcliffe Wagonway shortly after this time and this may have been the locomotive in question. The original Act provided for some loading of coal from the north pier and it is possible that the locomotive moved some wagonloads of coal over the viaduct as well as stone. Until the arrival of the first locomotive horses would have provided the principal motive power, though the location of the stables has not been discovered.

The coal was transported from the harbour by sailing ship; one of the earliest to use the port was the *Isabella*. Later this vessel was involved in transporting coal to, and lime from, the port at Holy Island.

An *Account of the Strata sunk through in the first pit at Radcliffe Colliery* is dated 5th November, 1839. At this time the shaft had reached a depth of 480 ft. The account showed that the shaft passed through various coal seams, some not commercially viable as a result of either their poor quality or the shallow depth of seam. The main seams mined were the Radcliffe Seam (sometimes referred to as the 'Northumberland Main' or 'High Main Coal') at 140 ft, the Prince Albert Seam at 226 ft, the Queens Seam at 340 ft, the Little Wonder Seam at 370 ft, the Princess Seam (or Top Seam) at 440 ft and the Duke or Main Seam at almost 480 ft. All of these were over two feet thick, the widest being the six feet Radcliffe Seam. Ten horses were employed underground to haul the coal tubs.

The early success of the venture can be gauged by the coal export figures from Amble. A total of 79,500 tons were reported as leaving the port in 1840. Other figures illustrate the amounts of coal drawn over the wagonway. In 1837 some 375 chaldrons (a chaldron is about 18 tons) of coal were drawn with 26 chaldrons of 'best coal' and 136 chaldrons of 'smalls' being used for landsale. By the end of 1838 this had risen to a total of 3,642 chaldrons. In 1841 a second shaft was opened and by 1842 the first shaft (referred to as 'A Pit') had produced 3,666 chaldrons and the second (referred to as 'B Pit') 5,573! The increase in coal traffic necessitated the purchase of 12 additional wagons from Killingworth. 'A Pit' closed in 1843 but 'B Pit', now to its full depth, continued to increase its output, this rising to 11,491 chaldrons in 1845. Later the values were quoted in tons, the figure for 1854 being over 20,000 tons. In 1843 coal was reported as being transported to the staithe (for export), sold at the colliery (landsale coal), sold to agents or workmen, sold for use on steam boats, for use at the carbon works, and for use at a local limekiln. The best coal was shipped at 17s. per chaldron with small coals fetching 7s.

The increase in the local population up to 724 by the date of the 1841 census was largely caused by the increase in size of the quarrying and mining community. In June 1838 between 40 and 50 pitmen were employed; however, by 1840 there were some 150 hewers and putters alone. The houses for the colliers, located close to the Radcliffe Colliery, and for the contractor's men, near the quarry and harbour, were reportedly very poor, some being of wood and earth construction.

The year 1844 proved to be an eventful one. The 'local' miners went on strike, largely as a result of their dissatisfaction with the way that coal was being weighed, and the management brought in some Cornish 'blacklegs' to take over the working of the pit. This caused much local controversy. By the end of that year just 5,650 chaldrons of coal had been moved though by the end of 1845 the figure had risen to nearly 11,200. There was some further unrest in 1847 when the management had a scheme for just 1 in 4 tubs of coal raised to the surface to be weighed (wages depended on weights) but by 1853 all tubs were weighed thus ensuring fairness.

Also in 1844, and as a result of the need for better facilities for moving the coal from the port, the Warkworth Harbour Commissioners proposed further improvements to the harbour for loading coal for export and for unloading of stone from ships arriving in ballast plus some dock facilities. The plans were once again drawn up by Rennie (dated 29th November, 1844) and the contractors, Kingscote & Brown, were appointed. Their work involved the construction of new staithes, extension and improvements to the North and South piers, building railways associated with the works and also '...engine houses, workshops and cottages used in connection with the construction works'. In reality many of the workmen were still housed in '...links and huts raised by sods'. The work was completed by 1849 at a cost of £100,000 for the North Pier and £16,000 for the South Pier. The new staithes came into operation in that year.

The year 1849 was notable for the construction of the link between Chevington, on the Newcastle & Berwick main line (opened 5th September), and Amble. This was to provide a rail outlet to the national railway network for the Amble area collieries, especially the Broomhill Colliery. However, much of the coal continued to leave via the harbour, and the Radcliffe Wagonway remained busy.

It was in 1852 that the Radcliffe Colliery was to suffer its first fatality when a fall of coal killed a 70-year-old miner. Three further deaths, caused by mineral falls, took place in the 1850s and four more in the 1860s, though one of the last occurred when a boy fell in the shaft. At this time the colliery was described as having '...pit shafts, waste land and engine houses, machine houses, screens, railways, crabs, gins, sheds, workshops, buildings, pond, yards and appurtenances'.

In the 1850s the ownership of the colliery was assumed by, firstly, Joseph & John Harrison and then, after a brief period of inactivity in 1854, by Harrison, Carr & Co. (also involving a gentleman called Carl Lange) who operated it until 1875; they were often referred to simply as the owners of Radcliffe Colliery. The population and importance of Amble continued to rise: to 1,040 in 1851 and to 1,275 in 1861. In 1860 the colliery was producing some 60,000 tons of coal per annum. The First Edition Ordnance Survey maps show the Radcliffe Colliery and the line of wagonway leading to the staithe at the harbour. Near to the staithe there was a runround loop to facilitate wagon handling and for storage of empties. A 'coal depot' is marked near to the water's edge. To the south of the line, at the colliery entrance the wagonway forked, with one track passing to each side of the main colliery building with the shaft and winding gear. The two lines met up on the opposite, south, side of the plant. Two sidings passed beneath the loading screens and one additional siding, to the west of the complex, served an engine shed or workshop.

A company, known as the Warkworth Harbour Dock Co. was set up by Act of Parliament in 1851, shares in which were purchased by Harrison, Carr & Co. In January 1855 the NER agreed to sell the Radcliffe company a 2-4-0 steam locomotive, numbered 60 (built by Charles Tayleur's company at Vulcan Foundry in 1839); it is not known whether the sale actually proceeded. A Board of Trade report of about 1873 refers to a boiler explosion that may refer to this locomotive or to another locomotive such as the small saddle tank mentioned earlier.

In 1875 Harrison, Carr & Co., aware of a decline in coal production, disposed of their harbour interests to a certain Hugh Andrews of Belfast whilst the colliery was sold (in the same year) to a Mr Andrews and then to Haggie, Smith & Co., who operated it under the name of the Radcliffe Coal Co., a concern registered in Collingwood Buildings, Newcastle. They took out a lease for 53 years from January 1878. Fireclay started to be removed from the Radcliffe Colliery at this time in association with the developing brick and tile industry at Amble (q.v.).

A few years earlier, in 1869, Andrews had obtained the nearby Broomhill Colliery (NU248013) but sent coal in gravity-propelled trains along the NER line to Amble, with horses returning the empties. Andrews became the harbour proprietor and invested in further developments at Amble to facilitate this traffic. More land was reclaimed from the river, the river itself was straightened, more quays were built, dredging and blasting took place to deepen entrances and berths and new staithes replaced the originals. The South Pier was practically rebuilt. The output from Broomhill Colliery doubled and the growth of Amble mushroomed as a result of his business acumen. Its population had passed the 2,000 mark by 1881! The harbour developments allowed the berthing of larger sailing ships and steamships, the first steamer having arrived in 1870 to take away 400 tons of coal. The increasing output from Broomhill probably contributed to the decline in output from Radcliffe.

Contemporary documents show that Radcliffe Colliery had an engine house, agents house, workshops, office, coal sheds and five shafts. A deepening of the harbour took place between 1882 and 1884, and further new quays were constructed in 1883-84. The contractor employed was Alfred Thorne of Cannon Street in London who extended the various railways on the piers and introduced his own crane for the lifting of stone and cement. He also employed a steam-powered stone breaker. Around this time there were proposals for creating a £1½ m 'National Harbour of Refuge' at Amble with breakwaters extending out to sea from the Birling Links (level with the village of Warkworth) and from near to Hauxley Point. Plans were drawn up by the Civil Engineers, Thomas Meik & Sons of Edinburgh, but nothing came of this scheme.

Around this time the Radcliffe Coal Co. obtained some new motive power for its wagonway, staithes and sidings. The first locomotive was an Andrew Barclay 0-4-0 saddle tank (Works No. 147 of 1873) whilst the second was another Barclay (No. 663, built in 1890 and named *Radcliffe No. 2*). The locomotives hauled their trains of wagons to the foot of the inclines leading to the staithes. They would then run around and push the wagons to the top of the slope. Individual wagons were then run to be unloaded by gravity under the supervision of a 'teemer'.

For a few years the harbour commissioners had felt that there was a need for further protection from the north-easterly storms. Accordingly in 1890 the North Pier was even further extended and, after failure of the appointed contractors, the commissioners' own men finished the work. The total cost was £¼ million. Radcliffe Middle Staithe was deepened by Engineers Thomas Meik & Sons. By 1898 when the extension was complete, and after the commissioners had purchased their own hopper-dredger, the harbour could accommodate vessels of 1,400-1,500 tons. Loading of coal could take place at a rate of between 200-500 tons per hour.

By the early-1890s one of the sidings, formerly passing under the loading screen gantry at Radcliffe had been extended southwards, then eastwards, to form a through line to the new pit known as Newburgh Colliery. One other siding remained beneath the screens at Radcliffe. The track to the west side of the main colliery building was modified to form a loop, with a short siding leading to the shed or workshop.

However, by then the fortunes of Radcliffe Colliery were in marked decline as a result of rock faulting and in 1892 coal extraction from the pit ceased. Until that time the pit had been making a small profit and continued doing so until 1894 when the profit, from the sale of stockpiled coal, sank to just £2,774. The pit officially closed on 18th April, 1894, though there was some landsale of coal

The year is 1900 and a steamer eases towards the Amble quayside behind a moored barge possibly to receive a load of coal from the wooden-sided hopper wagons on the staith.

Ken Middlemist Collection

The Newcastle-registered collier, *Hauxley*, is manoeuvred towards the Amble harbour entrance by a steam paddle tug. On the south jetty several well-dressed 'locals' are getting some sea air. The headshunt of one of the railway sidings is on the right-hand side of this undated picture.

Author's Collection

until 1st September of that year (for example 198 tons in the last fortnight). Perhaps surprisingly a new locomotive, Barclay 742/1894 called *Lyne*, arrived at the site. Another locomotive believed to have arrived at Radcliffe was an 0-4-0 saddle tank from Haggie & Company of Gateshead. Its identity has not been confirmed but it is alleged to have been originally built by the Black Hawthorn or Lowca Works.

A new link was made at Amble between the Radcliffe Wagonway and the NER line in 1893 for Broomhill Colliery purposes. The accounts for the years 1895 and 1896 recorded a loss despite the disposal of some of the plant. The locomotive shed at Radcliffe was closed and the engines were first moved to the new pit opened to the south-east at Newburgh, where, in 1895, they were valued at £1,600. Later they were further moved to Broomhill. In 1895 plant still at Radcliffe consisted of the pumping engine, winding engine, jack engines, a hauling engine, pulleys and a Worthington pumping engine, with a total value of £636. These were, somewhat mysteriously, described as 'still in use' (perhaps still in working order). By 1898 some of the plant may have been disposed of for the value of remaining items was quoted as £500; alternatively the lower value may have simply reflected their depreciation in value. The colliery sidings were taken up and the rails were disposed of in 1896. By 1900 the Radcliffe firm was absorbed into the new Broomhill Colliery Ltd, which operated both the Broomhill Pit adjacent to the NER line (NU248013) and the new Newburgh Pit (NU278020).

In 1895 over half a million tons of coal were shipped from Amble and its population had risen to over 4,000! The rail approaches to Amble were through an area in which new houses and works had being established.

No. 28 was one of the last NCB steam locomotives employed at Amble and as such featured in a large number of photographs. Here it crosses high over Percy Street as it returns a rake of hopper wagons back from the staiths towards the British Rail exchange sidings.   *Jon Marsh*

It is 1st February, 1961 and the points are set for this hopper wagon to leave the NCB Staith, having just discharged its load of coal into the hold of a coastal steamer below. The 21 ton hopper wagon was the most common rail vehicle in the Amble area.

Beamish Museum Collection

The date is 20th June, 1966 and the Radcliffe Staith at Amble is free of wagons. By this time Hauxley Colliery was approaching its closure date and traffic from the local collieries was almost at an end.   *Beamish Museum Collection*

Early in its history the Broomhill company owned steamships which included the SS *Ringwood*, the SS *Turrethill* and the SS *Broomhill*, though there were a large number from other companies also involved in shipping coal from Amble. The later Broomhill vessels included the SS *Amble*, SS *Chevington* and SS *Bondicar*. These were loaded at what became Amble staithes Nos. 4 and 5 (staithe 5 was known as the 'Radcliffe Staithe' and was the oldest of the five). The Broomhill company's vessels had their main superstructure, bridge and funnel mounted centrally so that the two holds were fore and aft of this. No. 5 staithe would load the fore hold, whilst No. 4 would load the aft hold with the vessel facing towards the sea. Because of the nature of the staithes the coal was discharged into the holds from just one hopper wagon at a time from each of the two staithes. Discharge was via the ends of the wagons. The other Amble staithes could discharge coal from up to three wagons at a time. The coal was exported to the mainland of Europe and as far around the British coastline as Devonport.

A newly-arrived Barclay saddle tank locomotive (849/1899) called 'No. 3' was transferred into the ownership of the Broomhill company. Around the same time the *Glasgow Herald* advertised for sale from here an Andrew Barclay locomotive with 12 in. cylinders. This is presumed to have been No. 663 despite it actually having 11 in. cylinders.

Trains of coal from Broomhill were now moved to the staithes using the former wagonway by means of the newly laid connection through the Radcliffe site, then via a new connection at Amble to the Broomhill staithes. (All coal arriving at the Radcliffe staithes from the Broomhill collieries was subject to wayleave payments if it had to cross over the NE/LNER and later BR tracks at Amble.) The newly-laid connection was constructed after delays had been caused to colliery trains working over the NER's line by the NER's own passenger trains, and traffic from the new Togston Colliery to the south. However, the Newburgh, Broomhill and Togston pits were all located outside the Alnwick District boundary and so their history, partly covered in other publications, is not repeated here.

The large-scale Ordnance Map of the 1920s, marks Radcliffe Colliery as 'Disused' though one siding remains in place at the site at that time. The line to Newburgh, marked 'wagonway' is still shown with the addition of the branch towards Broomhill curving south-west, then west, towards that colliery.

Today almost all of the land formerly occupied by the wagonway, collieries and staithes is private property, though their positions can be discerned from nearby roads, without the need for trespass.

11 – The Hauxley Colliery Branch

In the first half of the 1920s the Broomhill Colliery Co. made the decision to open a new colliery at Hauxley (NU283034). It opened in 1926 and operated for 40 years, surviving nationalization but being closed by the National Coal Board on 25th November, 1966. In its early years the colliery produced steam coal, though later household coal and fireclay were produced additionally.

Just two more years of the export of coal from Amble remained when Broomhill-based locomotive No. 28 (HC1825/1949) was photographed shunting at Amble staiths. The locomotive had only just over one more year of life, being scrapped in January 1970.

Dave Dunn Collection

Part of Amble's extensive fleet of fishing boats is tied up beneath the Hauxley and Broomhill Staith on the south side of Amble Harbour. The absence of activity may suggest that this photograph was taken on a Sunday.

Beamish Museum Collection

Hauxley Colliery was a brand new pit and therefore not encumbered with the workings or remains of earlier pits on the site. It was thus built on 'modern' lines with well-proportioned underground galleries and good ventilation. Underground there was a 2 ft gauge railway with large capacity (25 cwt) tubs fitted with roller bearings to reduce maintenance. The use of electric motors to haul the tubs on cables greatly reduced the need for ponies in the pit. State of the art cutting equipment and conveyors made this an efficient pit.

By 1930 coal was being won from the Albert, Bottom, Duke, Princess, Queen and Radcliffe seams, then later the Bensham seam. By 1960 all of these were worked out and production concentrated on a new seam known as the Brockwell Seam which was the only one producing coal when the pit closed. The pit became part of the NCB Northern Division upon nationalization in January 1947. At this time it was producing some 54,000 tons of coal per annum. In the 1930s it employed over 675 men of whom over 80 per cent were working below ground. The number employed was less than one-third of this figure at the end of World War II though it rose to almost 600 two years before closure. Although the pit suffered no large scale disasters a total of 12 men lost their lives in accidents whilst the pit was owned by the Broomhill company. The colliery was eventually demolished, the pump house being the last building to survive.

Left: A Hauxley Colliery wagon label.
Beamish Museum Collection

Locomotive No. 33 was built at Vulcan Foundry as Works No. VF 5306/1945. It saw four periods of service at Broomhill and like WB 2757 worked the Hauxley branch. Its last move was to Whittle Colliery in 1969, being finally scrapped in March 1973.   *Beamish Museum Collection*

Locomotive No. 51, built by Bagnall as Works No. WB2757 in 1944, was a typical 'Austerity' design. It was based at Broomhill NCB shed and regularly worked trains on the Hauxley branch in 1964. This photograph was taken on 31st July of that year.   *Beamish Museum Collection*

The colliery was served by a branch line, laid with new rails, which was constructed from a junction with the line leading to the Radcliffe and Broomhill collieries on the alignment of the original Radcliffe Wagonway (still serving Newburgh and Broomhill collieries in the 1920s). The line swung eastwards just to the north of what is now the Amble sewage works. It approached the pit which had two arrival and two departure sidings. In addition two lines passed beneath the screens for wagons to be loaded. There was no engine shed at the colliery, the motive power being supplied from Broomhill Colliery which, by then, had a variety of locomotives available including 4- and 6-wheeled saddle tanks built by Andrew Barclay, R. & W. Hawthorn, and Hawthorn Leslie, plus other locomotives formerly owned by the London Brighton & South Coast Railway, and by constituents of the Great Western Railway. After nationalization the locomotives belonged to the National Coal Board's North Northumberland Area. Trains of up to 12 loaded wagons were worked from the colliery to the staithes at the port.

In 1954 the NCB abandoned the section of line between Broomhill Colliery and the Hauxley branch junction, thus bringing the movement of coal along much of the original Radcliffe Wagonway alignment to an end. Instead the coal from Broomhill was moved to Amble via the British Railways (former NER/LNER line). By 1970 coal export from Amble had ceased and the staithes had been demolished. The remains of the line from Radcliffe and Hauxley were grassed over and both housing and trading estates spread southwards from Amble.

Today, with the aid of a map, most of the route of the Hauxley Colliery branch can be discovered on the ground by examination of the layout of some of the new roads, by the outline of modern housing and industrial developments and by paths and field boundaries. It still shows up very clearly, as does the former colliery site, on recent aerial photographs.

12 – The Pier Railways and Craneways

Whilst it is accepted that the railways and craneways on the piers at Warkworth Harbour, Amble, were not built for the movement of coal it is appropriate to consider them here as the development, maintenance and protection of the harbour were vital prerequisites for the successful export of the coal from the local pits.

The 'Plan of the Township of Amble', surveyed by Sopwith & Scott of Newcastle and drawn in July 1840, shows the early railway line which was laid to carry stone for the building of the first piers or breakwaters at what was then called Warkworth Harbour at the mouth of the River Coquet. The land on which it was built was largely owned by the Duchess of Newburgh, but some, close to Pan Rocks, on the south side of the estuary, was owned by a Mr G. Smith. As first built the line started at a group of three short sidings at Pan Rocks between the high and low water marks. Later a new quarry was opened a short distance inland and the line was diverted to serve this. Leaving here the line hugged the line of high water mark until it reached the 'Braid', a low-lying muddy area. Here a series of wooden piles were sunk to carry the line over the River Coquet to its north bank. The description of the construction of this viaduct or 'platform'

This view, taken from a picture postcard, shows the craneway on the South Pier at Amble harbour. The crane is just visible, being stabled in its usual position adjacent to the Coastguard station.
Author's Collection

An unidentified paddle tug crosses Amble harbour towards Radcliffe staith. Note the crane working on the craneway and both steam- and sail-propelled vessels tied up at the quay.
Author's Collection

appears in Nicholas Wood's report quoted earlier. On the north side of the harbour the line was continued towards the site where the breakwater was being constructed. A small shed was built over the line at this point to house the small locomotive. A small siding existed at the beginning of the breakwater and then the line was extended onto the breakwater itself. On the south side of the Coquet a short siding led towards the site where the South Pier was being constructed. The whole of this railway was presumably taken up after the completion of the breakwater's construction or possibly after its reconstruction in the 1840s by which time the initial works had proved to be inadequate. The line is not shown on the First Edition OS maps which were surveyed some years later.

The Second Edition OS maps were surveyed around the time of the further elongation and improvement of the piers (as they became known) in the 1890s. In addition Meik & Sons' plan of the works, drawn up in the same decade, provides useful corroboration. On Meik's map the North Pier is marked with an 'Extension in Progress' and a line of rails is marked extending the full length of the pier with a passing loop near to the seaward end and a small siding where the reinforcement of the north face commences. At the base or start of the Pier a small spur extends towards the dunes (close to the building marked as the 'Rocket Apparatus House'). The line then curves southwards from the pier, terminating in two sidings, one of which served a wharf with a crane. The 1920s OS map shows lines still present on this pier, possibly as a double-track formation, one track serving each face. The rest of the layout is similar though no crane is marked at the quay, which, by this time, had been extended eastwards to form a new wooden North Jetty. This area did not receive another full survey until after World War II by which time all traces of the lines had disappeared.

On the south side of the Coquet all traces of the original railway had disappeared by the 1860 survey. By 1895 the short South Pier had been constructed though the OS map does not show the existence of rails. However, two photographs taken in 1905 clearly show a rail-mounted mobile crane on the South Pier, seemingly on a broad gauge track. One shows the pier in an early stage of being extended whilst the other, taken in October, shows the work in a more advanced state. The 1920s OS map shows the South Jetty in its completed form, having been lengthened in an easterly direction to meet up with, and be extended beyond, the South Pier. The line of craneway rails is shown linking a flat area to the side of the Coastguard station with the beacon on the end of the pier. The crane appears to have been stabled, when not in use, at the landward end of the craneway, adjacent to the Coastguard station. The line existed into the early 1950s but was then removed with the Pier becoming a footpath.

By 1970 the water-filled quarry at Pan Rocks had been drained and filled in becoming converted into a recreation area. Repairs to the breakwaters in 1984 used stone from Howick Quarry, to the north-east of Alnwick. The Harbour Office at Amble still bears a brass plaque bearing the name of the Warkworth Harbour Commissioners and at least one boundary stone, marking the edge of the harbour property, survives near to Pan Rocks. Except on stormy or windy days the piers can provide residents and visitors with stimulating places for exercise, though access to the North Pier requires a long walk along the beach or through the dunes from Warkworth!

The Colliery, Longframlington.

This old commercial postcard shows Longframlington Colliery before the construction of the cableway to Whittle. At this time all of the colliery's coal was taken away in horse-drawn carts like those shown in the picture.

John Ryan Collection

This is the loading terminal at Longframlington Colliery with a filled tub just leaving. Just one lad was responsible for the attachment of the loaded tubs onto the overhead cable.

'Colliery Engineering' courtesy of the Scottish Mining Museum

Chapter Six

The Colliery Railways and Cableways of Longframlington, Brinkburn and Ward's Hill

These cableways and railways form an arc, starting to the east of Rothbury at Longframlington, clockwise on to Brinkburn and then to Ward's Hill, south of Rothbury. All were for the transport of coal, though one line also transported ironstone. The cableways are included as they were considered to be alternatives to the building of railways or tramways, and in the case of the Longframlington line, it was colliery tramway 'tubs' that were moved along the overhead cableway.

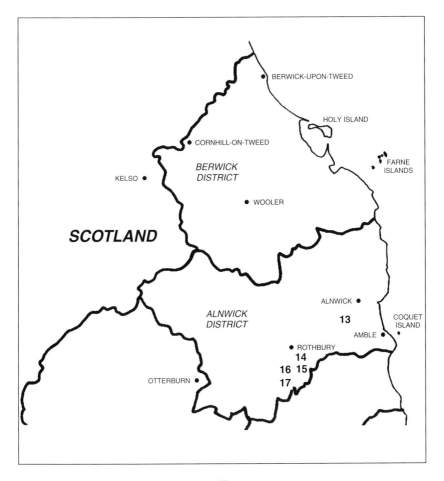

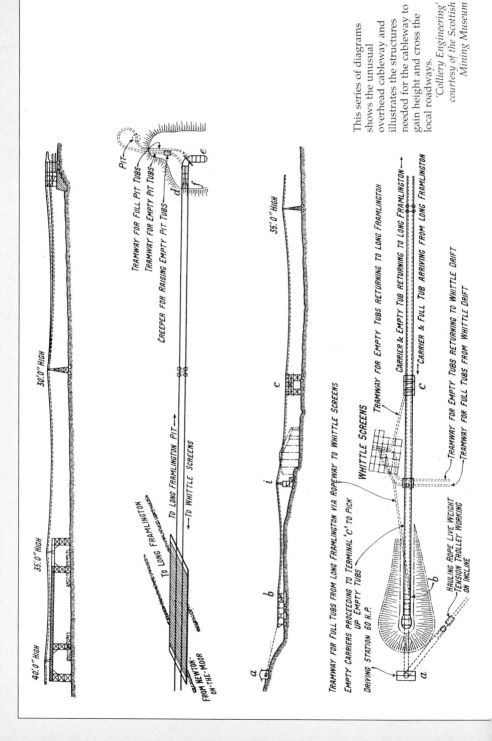

This series of diagrams shows the unusual overhead cableway and illustrates the structures needed for the cableway to gain height and cross the local roadways.

'Colliery Engineering' courtesy of the Scottish Mining Museum

40'.0" HIGH

35.0" HIGH

30'.0" HIGH

TRAMWAY FOR FULL PIT TUBS

TRAMWAY FOR EMPTY PIT TUBS

CREEPER FOR RAISING EMPTY PIT TUBS

PIT

d

e

f

To LONG FRAMLINGTON PIT →

← TO WHITTLE SCREENS

TO LONG FRAMLINGTON

TO LONG FRAMLINGTON

FROM NEWTON-ON-THE-MOOR

b

35'.0" HIGH

c

i

a

b

TRAMWAY FOR FULL TUBS FROM LONG FRAMLINGTON VIA ROPEWAY TO WHITTLE SCREENS

EMPTY CARRIERS PROCEEDING TO TERMINAL 'C' TO PICK UP EMPTY TUBS

DRIVING STATION 60 H.P.

WHITTLE SCREENS

TRAMWAY FOR EMPTY TUBS RETURNING TO LONG FRAMLINGTON

CARRIER & EMPTY TUB RETURNING TO LONG FRAMLINGTON →

← CARRIER & FULL TUB ARRIVING FROM LONG FRAMLINGTON

c

TRAMWAY FOR EMPTY TUBS RETURNING TO WHITTLE DRIFT

TRAMWAY FOR FULL TUBS FROM WHITTLE DRIFT

HAULING ROPE LIVE WEIGHT TENSION TROLLEY WORKING ON INCLINE

a

b

13 – The Longframlington Colliery Cableway

Longframlington Colliery, also known as Framlington Colliery or Framlington Pit, was located to the north of the village (at NU123025) adjacent to the road leading towards Newton-on-the-Moor and Alnwick. Prior to the opening of this colliery other small pits had operated in the Longframlington area. These had been landsale pits satisfying the needs of the local community. The Longframlington Colliery (locally known as the 'Nicholson Pit' after G. & W. Nicholson who sank the first shaft in 1862) was in full production by the 1870s. The seam varied between 28 and 34 inches in thickness and was some 320 ft below the ground surface. Its Manager at this time was a William Pattison. Five men worked above ground whilst 23 miners were employed below. The corresponding numbers for 1902 and 1908 were seven and 20, and six and 24 respectively. After the end of World War I the Longframlington Coal Co. was formed. Its Manager was a Mr W. Sergison. Later the South Shilbottle Coal Co. and then, finally, the Cooperative Wholesale Society Ltd owned the pit, the maximum number of men employed reaching about 65 in the early 1920s. The pit worked the Shilbottle seam until its final closure on 31st December, 1931 when almost 40 men were employed. At different times the pit produced coal for gas making, household coal, steam coal and manufacturing coal.

Coal was raised from underground in small tubs which had been loaded at the coalface. In the 1920s, instead of the screening of the coal being performed at Longframlington it was taken, first by road, to a central screening plant at Whittle Colliery, near Shilbottle, which lay adjacent to the Great North Road, some four miles away to the north-east. The road between the two locations was quite narrow and often in a poor state of repair. It was the Directors of South Shilbottle Collieries (1928) Ltd who considered how to solve the problem of the road transport of the coal to Whittle. Several alternatives were considered. That chosen, on the grounds of cost and efficiency, was the construction of an aerial ropeway. The equipment was erected by Messrs R. White & Sons of Widnes in Lancashire, who specialised in designing, building and erecting such systems. A 60 bhp engine provided the drive. The intermediate supporting towers and parts of the terminals were made of wood, except for the 'tensioning stations'. These tensioning towers were located at either end, and in the middle, of the system. These consisted of steel towers, the tension in the cable being created by the use of loaded rail trolleys running on inclines. At each end of the system was a network of rails for the movement of the tubs.

The capacity of the system was about 32 tons per hour, but the unusual feature was that instead of 'buckets' being used, the pit tubs themselves were used to carry the coal, this meaning that breakage of coal, during transfer from tub to bucket, could be eliminated. Attachment of the tubs to the overhead cables was entirely automatic at both ends of the system. A loaded tub would first engage with a carrier, and then descend by gravity along a rail line where it was raised to allow the carrier to engage the hauling cable. Each tub carried a load of about 6½ cwt. The speed of the moving cable was 330 ft per minute. On arrival of the tub at the far end of the 'line' the carrier was automatically released and it would stop by means of a spring buffer. The carrier, meanwhile,

Above: This picture shows the 'midway station' on the Longframlington cableway with an empty tub returning to the colliery. In the distance can be seen several of the standard pylons which carried the 'line' above the fields.

'Colliery Engineering' courtesy of the Scottish Mining Museum

Right: Here a tub is shown crossing the A1 Great North Road shortly before arrival at Whittle Colliery. The platform and fence protected vehicles on the road from possible falls of coal. The means of attachment of the tub to the cable is well illustrated.

'Colliery Engineering' courtesy of the Scottish Mining Museum

would progress around the loop and await an empty tub to return to the pit. The loaded tub itself then reversed direction and descended by gravity down an inclined plane to the discharge point. After emptying it ascended an inclined plane and rejoined the cableway for return to the colliery. On returning here the tub would be automatically released from the carrier (which progressed along ready to receive another loaded wagon) and would be taken up a 'creeper' to the banking level ready to be taken down the pit. Where the ropeway crossed roads, such as the Great North Road and the Longframlington to Newton road, a bridge of wire safety screens, mounted on latticework towers, was provided to prevent coal being discharged onto the highway in case of accident. The wooden and the steel towers were between 30 and 40 ft in height.

The whole handling of the cableway was as automatic as possible so as to reduce the associated labour charges. Only one man and two lads were required to work the entire system. The man attended to the driving gear whilst the lads looked after the dispatch of wagons at each end.

The Journal, *Colliery Engineering*, provided a description of the system in its November 1930 edition. Within 13 months of publication the system had closed, the pit being considered uneconomic. Many of the men transferred to Whittle Colliery. In the entire history of the pit there was just one fatality; it occurred on 7th January, 1866. The man concerned was walking backwards whilst carrying pit props to the head of the shaft. He slipped and fell down the shaft to his death.

After the closure of the pit, and before it was sealed, some local youths threw a firework into the shaft. This caused gas, which had built up since the closure, to ignite and a large explosion took place!

The colliery site is now private property and a caravan site is located nearby. A few of the former colliery buildings still survive at the site. Near to Swarland, towards the Whittle end of the cableway are the remains of some of bases of the overhead pylons, though these, and the rest of the cableway's route are on private ground. A local forester has reported that in the 1930s some damaged mine tubs were dumped at the edge of Swarland Wood close to the cableway alignment; he has suggested that these may have been associated with the cableway.

14 – The Healeycote Colliery Cableway

The Healeycote Colliery was located to the west of Longframlington, on the north side of the road linking the village with the Morpeth to Rothbury road, now the B6344, near Pauperhaugh (NU112005). The first pit in the area is recorded as having been worked by a Mr Fenwick as early as 1762. Fenwick is known to have sunk two shafts.

It was in 1919 that a local man, Mr R. Wood, of Kings Avenue, Morpeth, took out a lease on the colliery, 'in the Parish of Brinkburn', with the intention of winning coal from the Shilbottle seam, though it appears that some coal had been removed from the pit in the previous five years. A favourable inspection had been carried out by William Armstrong & Sons, a firm of surveyors and mining engineers. Borings had shown that in places the seam was between 3 and 4 ft in

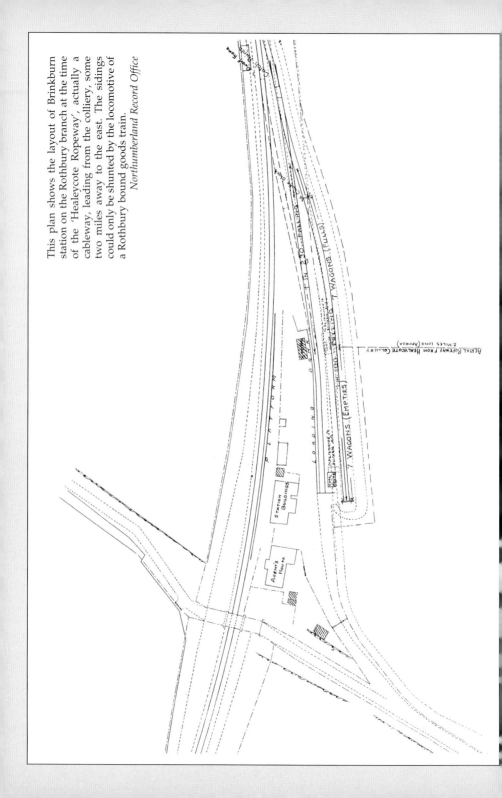

This plan shows the layout of Brinkburn station on the Rothbury branch at the time of the 'Healeycote Ropeway', actually a cableway, leading from the colliery, some two miles away to the east. The sidings could only be shunted by the locomotive of a Rothbury bound goods train.

Northumberland Record Office

depth. Elsewhere it varied from 2 ft 4 in. to less than a foot. Some of the coal was of good quality; some was very soft and friable. Many of the men employed at Healeycote had transferred from the nearby collieries at Chirm and the Lee when they closed. Initially there were 11 miners and four surface-men but by the mid-1920s just over 20 men were employed at Healeycote. Just fewer than 50 were employed at the time of the pit closure in May 1935. The Manager of the pit at closure was an Arthur Wood who may have been related to the lessee. It would appear that two shafts were sunk, one of 11 ft 6 in. diameter, one of 6 ft diameter (the latter being the ventilation shaft). The roof of the coal workings was sound, being of 18 inches of bluestone. However, above this was over 6 ft of limestone which contained large quantities of water which had always proved a problem for mines near this location. Pumps were needed to remove the 14 gallons of water per minute which would enter the pit on its east side. A Sullivan electric cutter was used at the coal face.

The pit was located adjacent to a minor road and was about two miles away from the nearest railway, the Rothbury branch of the North British Railway (NBR), later part of the LNER and British Railways. Because the pit was located at an altitude of some 310 ft and the railway was at nearly 350 ft at Brinkburn station (NU087995), two miles away, the building of a self-acting incline was an impossibility. The intervening river valley was at an altitude of about 150 ft and thus a mineral railway would have involved steep gradients, costly earthworks and a bridge over the river. Finally the roads between the pit and the branch railway were narrow and poorly made. Woods thus took the decision to link the pit and Brinkburn station by means of an 'aerial ropeway'. Brinkburn station was located 21.8 miles from Morpeth and 10.8 miles from the junction at Scots Gap.

The 'ropeway', actually using a continuous overhead steel cable, was approximately two miles long. No figures for the height of the supporting piers have been discovered though they were described in one document as 'of moderate height'. Apparently there was insufficient tension in the cable and there was a considerable degree of 'sag' between the piers when filled tubs were passing! Several tree plantations lay on the direct route between pit and station and it was necessary to cut 'passages' or 'rides' through parts of Hag Wood and Pauperhaugh Wood on the east side of the river and smaller woods below West Row on the west side. The ropeway followed the north side of Hag Wood for part of its length. After descending to the Coquet valley it rose up the steep hillside on the west side.

At Brinkburn the single-track NBR branch was located on a curve following the contours of the hillside. Brinkburn station platform was about 70 yards in length. To facilitate the cableway access to the site a tool house and coal house behind the station building were demolished. To the north-east of the platform was located the small goods yard with two sidings of about 100 yards in length. Originally there had been just one siding (on a gradient of 1 in 230) leading to a loading dock, the second, outer and more easterly siding being provided later specifically for the coal traffic. These sidings were operated by means of a 'dwarf' ground frame, all coming under the control of Rothbury station. Catch points and a 'choke block' protected the branch from wagons rolling out of the sidings. A small store was erected on the loading bank.

This picture shows the diminutive size of the station at Brinkburn. The sidings and discharge point of the Healeycote cableway are behind the fence at the rear of the station platform.

'Photos from the Fifties' courtesy of Hugh Davies

Taken from the railway overbridge this is Brinkburn station in 2009. The station building is on the right and the sidings and terminal of the overhead cableway were on the far right beyond the gable end of the building. The station is now a private house.   *Author*

Coal was delivered into wagons by means of chutes next to the coal siding. All shunting, i.e. the bringing of empty wagons and removal of loaded ones was performed by the locomotive of the local goods train when heading towards Rothbury, that is, in the down direction on the branch. Any resorting of the order of the train's wagons would be done at the yard at Rothbury. The coal siding at Brinkburn was permitted to hold seven wagons (*see plan on page 100*).

The pit and its cableway appear to have worked with some limited success through the late 1920s and early 1930s; a new shaft was sunk in 1930. At the time of the General Strike the pit, being privately owned and operated, remained open, the only one to do so in the area. Although miners from other pits arrived at Healeycote to attempt to encourage the miners to cease work, their attempts to approach the pit were thwarted by the efforts of a small number of the local constabulary whose 'bluffs' convinced the visiting miners. The policemen pretended that a much larger force of armed police were guarding the pit than was actually the case! In the event the removal of coal via the cableway negated the efforts of the visiting miners to form an effective picket line and the direct delivery of the coal to the railway meant that the LNER could continue to receive coal from a Northumberland pit! For their own safety the Healeycote miners made their way between their homes and the pit across the local fields so as to avoid the men on the picket lines.

Some coal was led, by cart and later by motor lorry, from the pit to the inhabitants of Longframlington village by Messrs Dodds & Robinson. Local lore suggests, however, that some of the locals obtained their coal by the alternative means of rocking or tipping the coal tubs as they progressed along the cableway. The spilled contents were gathered up and smuggled to local houses!

An inspection of the pit was made in 1934 by a Mr W.E. Lishman who reported that the pit could not continue to work economically. Another report, by a Mr F.C. Fallowes, recommended immediate closure, with just one encouraging statement that the sale of plant would meet liabilities. A mineral valuer, Mr Davies, concurred with the closure proposals but said that the plant had scrap value only. In practice the pit had started to lose money on its operations. In the last fortnight of its operation the total wage costs had amounted to £250 contributing to a total operating loss for the same period of £333.

Woods' shafts were filled in, steps being taken to ensure no subsidence, the plant and machinery were sold, and the site was cleaned. About one acre of land could not be restored for agriculture including the spoil tip which was located in the wooded valley of the Healeycote Burn.

Closure of the pit and the aerial ropeway officially took place on 7th May, 1935. However, on a later occasion the pit (or a new shaft at the site) was reopened and some coal continued to be won until about 1960. This coal was removed from the pit by road. The out-of-use ropeway had been totally removed by about 1950. On closure some of the men moved to Whittle Colliery. Today the colliery site can be identified via a track from the road but it is located on private land. Remains include the spoil tips and the concrete bases of both the pit winding gear and the gantries at the end of the ropeway. The Rothbury branch line closed on 11th November, 1963 (the last goods train ran a couple of days earlier) and Brinkburn

Several large concrete slabs, some with fixing bolts still in place, are the remains of the bases of the pylons and pit gear at the colliery end of the Healeycote Colliery Cableway. The site is now littered with dumped agricultural items.   *Author*

The spoil tip of the former Healeycote Colliery survives adjacent to the Healeycote Burn which was formerly used for washing coal. At present the burn, on the far side of the tip in this photograph, is eroding its base making it increasingly unstable and dangerous.   *Author*

station, a part of the trackbed and the area of the former sidings were sold into private ownership. Today they form a private residence and garden to which there is no public access. The station site can be viewed from the overbridge on the nearby lane which is a public right of way.

15 – *The Brinkburn Colliery and Ironworks Wagonway*

The Brinkburn Ironworks (NZ 104993) was located on the Brinkburn Estate to the south of the road leading from Weldon Bridge to Rothbury, to the east of the hamlet of Pauperhaugh. It operated briefly in the 1850s. A plan of its smelter furnace exists in the Northumberland Record Office. It smelted iron obtained partly as nodules from a band of clay-ironstone, and partly from shale beds, both being obtained from pits located a small distance to the north. These beds alternated with beds of sandstone, fireclay and small coal seams. The nodules, on analysis, were shown to have a respectable iron content, 37.70 per cent of iron, comparable to the iron deposits found at Redesdale and Hareshaw (near Bellingham). The bands of iron in the shale beds were shown to have an iron content of between 33 and 44 per cent. The pits have sometimes been referred to as the Healey Pits (not to be confused with the much later, but nearby, Healeycote, or Healey Cote Colliery), but one surviving document refers to them as Longlands Pits. A recent industrial archaeological survey of the ironworks site revealed the remains of various stone buildings, and the base of a chimney, likely related to the blowing engine and boiler house. There was evidence of slag heaps indicating that iron had been smelted at the site. The possible site of the furnace was identified during the survey.

The pits were located to the west of the road from Pauperhaugh to Longframlington adjacent to the track leading towards High Linn (NU 109001 and NZ 107999). The former is marked on the First Edition OS maps as having two shafts, one for coal and one for ironstone and coal. The second, towards the south-west, has a single shaft marked but with an engine house and associated pond. Spoil tips existed to the north-west of both shafts.

Linking the pits to the ironworks was a wagonway which headed south-westerly in a straight line towards the Ironworks. Initially the line was fairly level, but further on it descended more steeply crossing the Rothbury road immediately before entering the works. Altogether the line descended about 100 feet from pits to works. No wagonway sidings are shown on the map though the shape of the tips close to one of the pits, plus on-site examination, suggests that some of the spoil may have been dumped from a siding or branch of the line. Examination of the width of the surviving wagonway embankments suggest that it was of narrow gauge though no documentary evidence confirms this. The line was almost certainly horse-drawn.

Only a small amount of documentary evidence relating to these pits, the wagonway or the Brinkburn Ironworks has survived. Fortunately, on 19th October, 1860, one of the local newspapers, the *Alnwick Mercury* contained a brief article about the works:

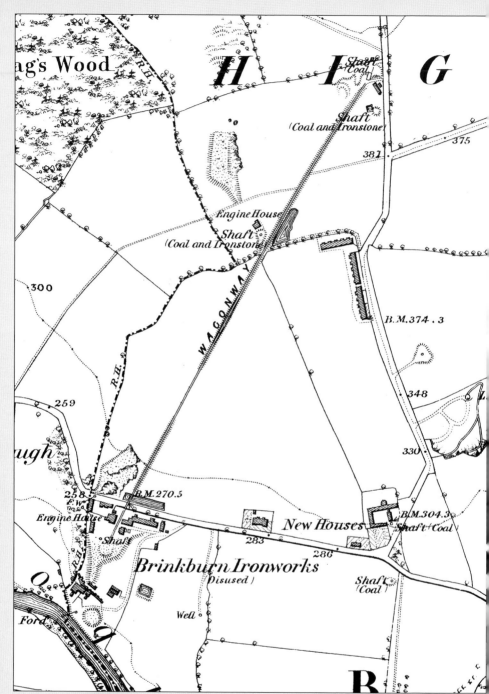

At least three shafts provided the coal and iron ore for Brinkburn Ironworks. The wagonway transported these raw materials directly to the works located to the south of the Morpeth to Rothbury road. Several other coal shafts were located nearby.

The Brinkburn coal and iron works, after a lingering existence of about four years, have at last become defunct. This is much to be regretted......
Limestone of excellent quality abounds. Iron ore also. The iron ore is of the nodular kind, being found in balls in a matrix of clay and blue shale. The bed where this ore is found varies from 13' to 18' in thickness. As we understand the yield of iron from the ore was 45%. Coal also abounds on this Estate, two seams are being spoken of: one 3' in thickness and the other 2'. This coal is reported to be of good quality for iron making and making good coke also.

This would indicate that the Ironworks, and hence the wagonway, operated from about 1856 to 1860. One document chronicles the visit of the works Managing Director with a certain Mr Bailey (possibly a land agent for the local estate) on 19th November, 1859. The cost of supplying the ironstone to the works had risen to 10s. 6d. per ton and at that price it was not financially viable to produce iron. It has also been suggested that the competition from cheaper Cleveland ores was too great and that the lack of a good means of transport of the site's end-products were contributory factors. The Director asked to be able to relinquish the lease on the site: 'I thought it would come to that sooner or later'. Some evidence suggests that the furnace at the ironworks was fired briefly in 1871, possibly in an attempt to reopen the works.

Just before the time of closure of the ironworks the route of a proposed railway line from Morpeth to Rothbury was being debated. The engineers, Messrs Joseph Locke and J.B. Errington, quoted the existence of the ironworks as being a good reason for the building of the line and an extension towards the North British Railway at Roxburgh. However, the building of the Rothbury branch came too late to save the works.

The locations of the coal and iron pits which supplied Brinkburn Ironworks are easy to spot from nearby roads. This photograph shows part of the surviving embankment of the Brinkburn Ironworks wagonway between the two mine sites. *Author*

This photograph, taken from the site of the winding engine at the Lee Sidings, shows the route of the former tramway. Lee Colliery was located where the trees form the skyline in the centre, with some of the colliery cottages on the left. The tramway embankment passed to the left of the two trees in the middle distance. In the foreground it rose towards the winding engine alongside the boundary fence, where, after a dry spell the grass adopts a yellowish shade. *Author*

Today all of the surviving evidence of the pits, wagonway and ironworks lies on private land. The locations of both of the pits are visible from the local roadways and the ground can be seen to be coloured black with the coal spoil. The line of the wagonway heading towards the Ironworks, which is also visible in part from the road, can be followed, initially on a shallow embankment, across the fields. Various remains exist at the site of the ironworks itself, identified during the archaeological survey.

16 – The Lee Tramway

The Lee Tramway was a short-lived double-tracked tramway linking Lee Colliery (NZ088977) with Lee Siding (NZ077983) on the Rothbury branch of the NBR, later the LNER. Lee Colliery was opened on both sides of the road leading from Longhorsley to the Rothbury to Scots Gap road (now the B6342) at Garleigh Moor. Lee Siding received its name when, in 1877, a siding was put in by the NBR, so that coal from nearby Lee Bridge Colliery could be taken away by rail. The coal was brought from the colliery by horse and cart operated by a Mr Caisley and loaded onto rail wagons at the siding. The siding's closure and removal in the 1890s followed on from the closure of this colliery but the name of 'Lee Siding' remained for the house adjacent to the siding.

Towards the end of the second decade of the 20th century Messrs Noble and Embleton formed a concern called the 'Brinkburn Colliery Company' and took out a lease for a new colliery at The Lee, to mine coal from the 'Hazon' or 'Chirn' seam. This produced first-rate coal for household purposes, though later it was the Shilbottle seam that was worked. The pit's first Manager was a Mr W. Wilson, later replaced by George Platten and finally, for the last few years of the pit's existence, by George Dixon. In 1921 seventy men were employed at the pit, including 44 below ground. By 1924 the number had increased to 83 (with 62 below ground). Much money was invested in the sinking of the pit and into providing accommodation for its workers, the nearby Embleton Terrace being constructed for the miners and their families. Ironically, this was only completed at the time that the pit closed. The landowner of the colliery site was the Duke of Northumberland of Alnwick Castle, and a standing rent of £30 per annum and a royalty of 5d. per ton of coal won was agreed with his office.

In 1917 the company had investigated, with 'Messrs Ropeways Ltd', the possibility of the construction of an aerial ropeway to link the pit and railway. In the event nothing came of this scheme and a double-tracked tramway was laid as an alternative. This was just over 1,400 yards in length.

The colliery, almost always referred to as 'Lee Pit', had its coal shaft and principal buildings to the south side of the Longhorsley-Garleigh Moor road. The air shaft, solely for ventilation purposes, was to the north of the road in the field next to the tramway, opposite the cottage still known as the 'Gussett'. The spoil tip lay to the west of the coal shaft on the same side of the road as the 'Gussett'. Two tramway tracks are shown on maps as leaving the main colliery site and crossing the road before curving sharply to the west to join the tramway proper. Its route followed a north-westerly direction, mainly on a

At the site of the Lee Siding can be found the brick base of some of the winding equipment used to haul wagons on the tramway. The site is located between the trackbed of the former Rothbury branch and the nearby road. *Author*

Near to the brick base of the former winding engine is a pile of scrap metal which purports to contain some of the former engine components. Shown here is a shaft fitted with gears and bearings which may be part of the old machinery. *Inset:* A close up showing the detail of the gear wheels at one end of the shaft. *(Both) Author*

fenced shallow embankment. It descended the hill, crossed a couple of field boundaries and Bog Burn, a tributary of the Forest Burn, before crossing over the main Forest Burn on a small bridge within the 'Lee Plantation'. A small footbridge, replacing an earlier ford, stood nearby. From here the line ran uphill as far as Lee Siding. It left the trees and, having crossed the minor road leading to Pauperhaugh, it curved sharply, entering the exchange yard. Here the line, which had become single just before the road crossing, split into two sidings, each leading to a small loading bank adjacent to the sidings from the Rothbury branch line. These two NBR sidings, 8.3 miles from Scots Gap, were in place by 1921. (Earlier a burn had been culverted beneath the sidings' site.) There was no loop on the branch at Lee Siding (as at Brinkburn station) but here only goods trains travelling in the up direction, i.e. towards Scots Gap and Morpeth, could stop to shunt the sidings, bringing empty wagons and removing full ones. The 'branch goods' stopped here on an 'as required' basis. The branch was on a steep gradient at this point and LNER diagrams show that a set of catch points was provided on the line in the direction of Rothbury to prevent any wagons escaping and accelerating down towards the terminus.

An electricity sub-station had been constructed by the Newcastle Supply Co. to provide electrical power for the winder at the mine shaft and it has been suggested that power was also supplied to an electric motor to drive the cable for moving the wagons along the tramway. No related documentation appears to have survived. No photographs of the tramway in operation have been discovered and it has thus not been possible to determine the type of wagons used, or how they were attached to, or detached from, the cable.

The early 1920s were not a happy time for the coal industry. Some markets were disappearing, many mines needed investment and the labour force was most unhappy with the threat of wage cuts. The Brinkburn Coal Co. made an effort to sell the Lee Colliery, as a going concern, to the Cooperative Wholesale Society for the sum of £12,500. This did not occur and the colliery was closed and abandoned in 1925. The Lee Tramway was thus short-lived.

Today the tree-covered colliery site can be identified by the irregular ground surface and remains of the spoil tips which discolour the ground. Embleton Terrace, the row of cottages built for the Lee miners, survives as a rather isolated linear hamlet. The line of the tramway, leading from the colliery, can be discerned as a result of the survival of its low embankment, although it is not identified on the latest OS maps. Though the trackbed lies on private land its course can be followed from adjacent roads. A rather overgrown public footpath leads from Lee

Remains of both the Winding House and some of the winding machinery survive at Lee Siding adjacent to the former Rothbury branch line. Here the identity of one of the Winding House bricks is revealed.   *Author*

Taken from the roadside opposite the Lee Farm, this photograph shows a length of the tramway trackbed as it climbs on an embankment towards the colliery site. On the left, just beyond the grazing sheep, a modern post and rail fence crosses the former alignment. A portion of one of the spoil tips can be seen on the far right.   *Author*

Some 40 years after the closure of the Ward's Hill drift mines and railways, the only surviving evidence of their existence is small, damp depressions in the hillside, plus the now grass-covered spoil tip from which this photograph was taken. The track, formerly used by lorries collecting coal from the drifts, is now occasionally used by a local farmer but is becoming less distinct.
                                                        Author

Ford, at the Forest Burn, through the Lee plantation. This crosses the former tramway route. From the Pauperhaugh to Lee Sidings road the former alignment can be seen climbing the hillside above the plantation. A slight ridge marks where the tramway formerly crossed this road. Right at the Lee Siding end of the line exist the remains of the former winding house and some possible components of the winding machinery. Beyond the house, still known today as 'Lee Siding', is the bridge which carries the Garleigh Moor road over the trackbed of the former Rothbury branch. This house has been formed from the combining of two cottages formerly inhabited by railway employees.

17 – The Ward's Hill Drift Railways

The coal seams on the west side of Ward's Hill had been worked by a local family, the Proudlocks, in the 1920s, and perhaps earlier by a Mr Brown who was also associated with the nearby limestone quarry. These were small scale operations with as few as three men being involved. The coal was for local household use. No railways were involved.

In the 1940s W.T. ('Willy') Bathgate decided to tap these coal seams which approached the surface on the opposite side of the road from his whinstone quarry. (Willy Bathgate was, at the time, extracting stone from a quarry on the opposite side of the Ward's Hill road and he was familiar with the local geology. He employed small locomotives in this stone quarry.)

Bathgate's main concern was to operate the lime kilns at Greenleighton a few miles to the south-west (see later volume) and it was for these kilns that most of the Ward's Hill coal was obtained. Road lorries were employed between Ward's Hill and Greenleighton. Because of the nature of the site the vehicles drove off the road down a gravelled trackway, and then performed a reversing manoeuvre before loading. They could then drive back up the steep track onto the road. Remains of this track survive today. Small drift mines, or adits, were excavated into the hillside (NZ079969). The seams dipped steeply and short narrow gauge rail lines were laid to facilitate removal of the coal and to take the waste to the hillside tip. The side-tipping rail wagons used on site were manhandled into and out of the adits; no locomotives or stationary engines were used. The remains of two of the adits can be seen today together with the spoil tips, which, although grass-covered, are easy to identify. The site is marked 'Colliery' on the OS maps published in the 1960s. At most, eight men worked on the site. Though most of the coal was transported to Greenleighton, small quantities were available for landsale. Towards the end of the site's coal operations in the early 1970s, some lorry loads of small coal were taken to Stella power station on Tyneside.

Access to the site is easy from the nearby Ward's Hill road and there is plenty of space to park a car safely at the side of the unfenced road. (One must beware of the cattle which are allowed to roam free in this vicinity. They seem to have a propensity for rubbing themselves against car wing mirrors!) The location of the approach track, the adits and their spoil tips can be inspected below the level of the road.

This photograph of the Forestburn Colliery and Quarry locomotive survives in the Barclay Archive in Glasgow. The locomotive's identity is AB 675/1891 and it is believed to have retained its former name of *Wingate* whilst at Forestburngate; by chance a hamlet, Wingates, was located a short distance from Forestburngate! With the landowner's permission it is possible to walk parts of the former line.
University of Glasgow, Andrew Barclay Archive

Chapter Seven

The Colliery Railways of Forestburngate, Ritton White House and Longwitton

18 – The Forestburn Colliery Railway

Forestburn Colliery (NZ 076968) and the nearby Forestburn Quarry (NZ 076966) were linked to the NBR's Scots Gap to Rothbury branch by a ¾ mile long standard gauge mineral railway. The colliery and quarry were located in Ravens Cleugh, not far from a quarry, which is in the valley of the Forest Burn. The sites, just a couple of hundred yards apart, were about 12½ miles south-south-west of Alnwick, not far from the Rothbury to Scots Gap road. The story of the colliery railway is described here, the quarry line being dealt with in a later volume.

The group of pits here had a short operational life, the first, to the north of the later rail-connected Forestburn Colliery, being operated from about 1871 until early in the 20th century. The recorded owners of these first pits were the Kirkheaton Colliery Co. (owners by 1910). These pits took coal from the Shilbottle Seam which came near to the surface at this point. Forestburn Colliery, the rail-served drift mine tapping the same seam, was opened in 1919 but was closed in 1923. It was owned by James D. Johnson (a coal merchant from Sunderland) until March 1921 when the Northumberland Collieries Ltd took over. (This company had been formed and incorporated in that year according to Companies House.) Later, a concern called the Northumberland Quarries Ltd took coal and stone from the site, probably still making use of the railway. This last company was never registered and may have been simply a convenient 'trading name'. The coal was used for household purposes.

Records show that the connection to the NBR was constructed and opened in 1919 and was located 19 miles and 38 chains from Scots Gap. The junction was just to the east of the bridge where the Scots Gap to Rothbury road (now the B6342) crossed the railway, not far from the Forestburngate public house (now 'The Gate'). The 'siding' lay to the south-east side of the line. It passed, almost immediately, through a gated fence and there was a loop of about 150 yards in length where empties could be left by the NBR/LNER branch engine, and full wagons of coal collected. It was normally traffic from down trains which served the siding, with up trains only calling 'as required'. A bench mark at the bridge is at 540 ft so the railway is probably some 20 ft lower at this point. A short spur or trap siding with a buffer stop was located to the south-east of the mineral line just beyond the loop and the points were presumably set to this direction when a NBR locomotive was using the sidings to prevent it progressing further down the line. A footpath crossed the line by the loop. From the loop, located in a field, the line headed in a south-easterly direction, until, on crossing the field boundary, it traversed a sharp 80 degree curve (close to the 500 ft contour) with its direction becoming almost north-east. Passing through two more fields on a gentle curve it emerged onto rough pasture and passed through the edge of Ravens Cleugh Wood. Soon after this a sharp 90 degree curve to the left brought the line back to a north-easterly direction. After passing the junction for the Quarry the line descended and entered the Ravens Cleugh Wood, crossing the Forest Burn by means of a small bridge downstream from a small waterfall, and then entered the colliery site located on the hillside above the burn. This was at about 450 ft above ordnance datum. At Ravens Cleugh Wood there was a junction with a short quarry branch which will be described in a later volume.

The quarry branch was also single-tracked and headed southwards from its junction with the colliery line. It crossed the Forest Burn by means of a small bridge and entered the quarry. The OS maps show no sidings on this line which was only just over 300 yards in length.

The line possessed its own steam locomotive which shuttled between the colliery and quarry, and the loop close to the NBR/LNER. It was an outside-cylindered 0-4-0 saddle tank built by Andrew Barclay of Kilmarnock (Works No. AB675/1891) which carried the name *Wingate*. It had previously been owned by the Wingate Limestone Co. of Wingate, Trimdon, County Durham.

Its Wingate Quarry was closed in the early 1920s and the locomotive had arrived at Forestburn by June 1921. The exact years of the locomotive's service at Forestburngate are not known. However, it is known that by June 1930 it had passed into the ownership of Shanks & McEwan Ltd, the civil engineering contractors, and was being used on their Farnsfield to Ollerton contract in Nottinghamshire.

No figures appear to have survived for the amount of coal produced at Forestburn Colliery. Just four men were employed when the pit was abandoned. After the closure and abandonment of the colliery in 1923, it was offered for sale with a scheme for an aerial ropeway to replace the mineral railway which must have proved very uneconomic to operate. This ropeway was never constructed and the last mineral products were removed by road.

Today a public bridleway leads from the Rothbury road across the private land to the south of Holling Hill and from this a footpath leads into Ravens Cleugh Wood, crossing the burn just to the north of the colliery site. Vegetation spoils the view of the former junction site from the surviving road overbridge nearby, though a former platelayers hut can be seen. 'The Gate' pub displays on the wall of its public bar some photographs of the Rothbury branch in operation, though, unfortunately, none showing the nearby mineral line in action.

19 – *The Whitehouse Colliery Tramway (near Ritton White House)*

Whitehouse Colliery (NU054947) was located to the north of Ritton White House, a farm and Bastle (defensive enclosure) situated ¾ mile to the east of the Scots Gap to Rothbury road (now the B6342) and about 15 miles south-west of Alnwick. A local gazeTteer of 1868, referring to both Ritton and Ritton White House, said that 'The inhabitants are chiefly engaged in the collieries'. It is possible that the miners, recorded as living at Ritton Colt Park, were mainly engaged at the small pits which were located close to the Rothbury road though they may have walked the ¾ mile to Whitehouse. There is no one listed in the 1871 census as resident at Ritton White House that is associated with the coal industry, all being connected with agriculture.

Whitehouse Colliery is not marked on the First Edition OS maps of the 1860s, but is clearly shown on those of the 1890s.

The first coal at Whitehouse was extracted via a vertical shaft. Later coal was removed from a drift mine tapping the Shilbottle seam to the north of the shaft. The 1881 census lists a William Gibson as an unemployed miner at Ritton White House, together with his sons, James, Robert and John, also described as miners, and it may be that they had worked, or were about to work, at Whitehouse Colliery. The first confirmed owners of the pit at Whitehouse were Francis and William Armstrong who also operated a limeworks at Hobberlaw, Alnwick. In an 1887 directory they are referred to as lime manufacturers and stone merchants at 'White House Lime Works', for they operated the nearby quarry and limeworks also. It is possible that they may have operated there since the 1870s according to some sources. Although the Whitehouse drift mine is described in 1888 and 1890 as producing landsale coal it is likely that it was the original source of coal for the limeworks. Certainly in 1896 and 1902 the drift was described as producing both household and 'manufacturing coal' and the nearby limeworks was working at this time. However, no other records appear to have survived which would confirm this.

The Whitehouse Colliery drift mine and shaft lay just to the east of the NBR's Rothbury branch. A line, marked 'Tramway' on the 1890s OS maps, is shown running from the site. The old shaft is marked at the side of the NBR line. The tramway ran parallel to the NBR Rothbury branch line (mostly in a cutting at this location) to an exchange dock on the headshunt for the NBR sidings, opposite the railway cottages (later called 'Daisy Cottages'). Here coal could be transferred to standard gauge wagons. The map is open to various interpretations at this point and it may be that the colliery tramway was extended in a south-easterly direction towards the limeworks. The tramway was horse-drawn and was about 700 yards in length.

In 1896 the colliery is known to have employed eight men, six underground and two working on the surface, this total, presumably including the men responsible for the operation of the narrow-gauge tramway. By this time the colliery had come under the ownership of the Ewesley Quarry Co., managed by a certain Matthew Taylor. Whitehouse Colliery finally closed on the 31st December, 1902 and it was officially abandoned the following day. It is assumed that the tramway closed around the same time. In its final years the colliery was worked only intermittently (there being no coal production in 1900 for example) and it was, apparently, in need of the injection of more capital if it were to have been developed further. John Longridge was the Manager at the time of closure; he was later to become associated with pits at Pelaw and Lambley. It was never reopened, identified on successive OS maps as an 'Old Drift'.

Today there are plenty of remains to be seen at the site. The position of the shaft is visible as a substantial hollow in the ground. Adjacent to this are the remains of the base of the winding engine. Nearby, the spoil tip contains some shale, fireclay and small pieces of coal. Leading southwards from the pit is the small tramway embankment (also exposing pieces of shale where the sides have been eroded by farm animals). The line of the tramway then enters a cutting whilst climbing a steep gradient for around 40 metres. At the top of gradient, adjacent to a rail-built fence post (no longer supporting a fence) and slightly to one side of the tramway's track alignment is what may have been, in the opinion of some local railway experts and an archaeologist, the base of a winding engine. Certainly a horse, or even a pair of horses, would have experienced difficulty in raising a loaded tub of coal up the gradient by direct haulage. A horse-powered winch with appropriate gearing would have facilitated the process. The remainder of the tramway trackbed, leading to the exchange sidings opposite 'Daisy Cottages', is now somewhat indistinct.

This choice of route for the tramway, involving a steep gradient up to a 'summit' is puzzling as an easier route could have been found by following the contours, though perhaps the construction of the boundary fencing adjacent to the Rothbury branch made this impossible in 1870.

On the left of the photograph is the steep incline leading from Whitehouse Colliery; after the 'summit' the line descended on a gentle gradient towards the exchange siding with the Rothbury branch, the trackbed of which is on the right of the picture.　　*Author*

The trackbed of the Rothbury branch is of at least double-width adjacent to the colliery and it may be that at some stage a siding was contemplated at this point to facilitate the loading of standard gauge wagons without the need for the use of the tramway. However, no documentary evidence of this has been discovered.

Today this site can only be approached via a public footpath which follows the private road from the B6342. Part of the former Rothbury branch standard gauge trackbed now forms the rather rough access road to the White House farm complex, and to the cottages, now called 'Daisy Cottages', adjacent to the site of the former Fontburn station. These cottages are occupied dwellings and access to them involves crossing private land. A recently built extension to Daisy Cottages resembles a railway signal box in outline! A signposted public bridleway from Coldrife, via Ritton Whitehouse to Newbiggin Farm, crosses the former Rothbury branch trackbed by means of a stone bridge very close to the Whitehouse Colliery site. These routes are marked on the latest OS maps.

20 – The Longwitton Colliery Railway

A casual visitor to this area at the start of the 21st century would be forgiven for believing that this had always been a rural backwater, yet it formerly possessed several small coal pits, then a colliery, quarries and a large limeworks! Later, in the 20th century, there was even an opencast pit not far from Longwitton station on the Rothbury branch.

Small-scale coal mining, in several small pits at Longwitton had taken place in the first half of the 19th century but it was not until the coming of the North British Railway's Scots Gap to Rothbury branch that the scale of local industry increased. The story of this branch railway line is told by Stanley Jenkins in his book *The Rothbury Branch* published by the Oakwood Press.

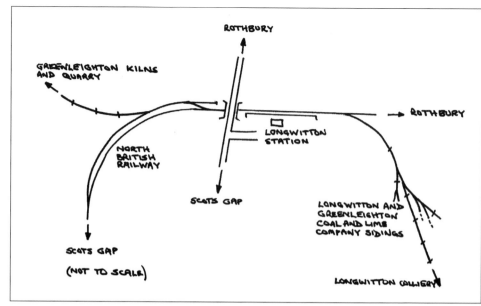

This plan of Longwitton station is based on one originating from *c*.1880, which shows the connections between the industrial lines to Greenleighton Limeworks and the Longwitton Colliery and the Rothbury branch line adjacent to Longwitton, formerly Rothley,station. *Author*

The embankment of the former branch to the colliery can be seen to the right-hand side of this view of Longwitton station on the NBR Rothbury branch taken from the road overbridge close to where the line formerly diverged towards the Greenleighton limeworks.

A.J. Wickens via Geoff Paxton

The following was reported in the local newspapers on 12th July, 1870:

The first train on the Northumberland Central Railway was run today. The Chairman of the Railway, Sir W.C. Trevelyan, Bart., and a number of other railway officials proceeded in a saloon carriage from Scots Gap to Rothbury, the natural beauty of the scenery being greatly admired.

At this time Sir Walter Trevelyan owned the whole of the local estate. Later it was to be split between Sir Charles Trevelyan (the Greenleighton lands) and Cecil Spencer Percival (those at Longwitton). A station was opened on the branch as 'Rothley' (NZ045908); this was originally a private halt for the Trevelyan Estate (based at Wallington Hall). Later, in 1873, it became a public station with a platform length of 70 yards, and was renamed 'Longwitton', though it was three miles away from the village of that name! By rail it was just over 3¼ miles from Scots Gap. It was to the east and west of this station that standard gauge lines were constructed to serve, respectively, the coal and lime industries which were to develop just a few years after the opening of the Rothbury branch.

It was in August 1874 that a lease was drawn up between the Wallington Estate and a consortium to be known as the Longwitton & Greenleighton Coal & Lime Co. The head of the consortium was William Bell, described as the colliery owner at Longwitton. The other members were Mr H. Robson (farmer), Mr Darnell (draper), Thomas Bonner (described as 'colliery owner, Longwitton', but who had also quarried lime at Greenleighton), Mr W. Robson (colliery viewer), Mr Denny (commercial traveller) and Mr Roscamp (mining engineer). Later Roscamp was to be involved at Shilbottle Colliery, near Alnwick. Mr Darnell was the company's first Chairman. This consortium planned to produce coal, limestone, common bricks and tiles, and also firebricks (using the deposits of ganister and fireclay found at the coal pit at Longwitton). They anticipated that half of the output from the colliery would be needed to fire the kilns, the rest of the products being for building use, agricultural use, for the chemical industry (in view of the products' purity) and the steel industry. The lease was to take effect from October 1874 and was planned to last for a period of 20 years. It permitted the company to lease about 100 acres of land and to build limekilns, railways and tramways. The railways were to be built from the Rothbury branch to both the colliery and kilns involving the laying of nearly 2 miles of rail of 'full gauge'.

The history of the lime industry at Greenleighton will be described in a subsequent volume. Here the story of the rail line of the Longwitton and Greenleighton Coal & Lime Co. Ltd, serving the Longwitton Colliery will be described. Strictly speaking the shaft and colliery buildings of Longwitton Colliery were a couple of hundred yards outside the Alnwick District, being just inside the boundaries of Castle Morpeth; however, the major part of the rail link and its junction with the Rothbury branch, was within the Alnwick boundary so can be dealt with here.

The colliery (NZ064896) was established about 1¾ miles south-east of Rothley, later Longwitton, station. It was located just to the north-east of Heugh House on the road to Longwitton village. Borings had taken place in the search for coal in 1772, 1807 and 1847. Numerous other small pits had operated nearby. Longwitton Colliery consisted of two shafts of 7 ft diameter, which were 40 yards apart, the older shaft being to the west. It was the east shaft which had the winding gear and cages. There was a 6 inch cylinder donkey engine present which pumped between 20 and 25 gallons of water per minute from the pit. In 1867 the colliery was in the hands of a Mr J. Bonner. It is recorded that in this year the total of coal mined in the Longwitton Pit, added to that produced at another nearby colliery known as the 'Law', was 20,000 tons, though the proportion obtained from each pit is not known.

The depth of the coal at Longwitton was 26 fathoms (156 ft) and the seam was 2 ft 6 in. thick at the bottom of the shaft, though the roof was said to be 'fragile' and needing careful propping. The colliery produced its first coal for the Longwitton & Greenleighton Co. in the year ending 13th May, 1875 when 2,981 tons were raised. In the next four years the amounts were 5,104 tons, 8,426 tons, 5,250 tons and 4,933 tons. In 1876 there were 13 hewers at work producing some 40 tons of coal and four tons of fireclay per day. By 1877 the coalface had reached 260 yards from the shaft onto some old workings and had gone beyond the boundary of the leased land by some 10 yards! Six hewers were at work producing about 25 tons per day and the mine was said to be in good order. However, trade was poor. By this time the 'Brinkburn Seam' was about 3 ft 4 in. thick. It was underlain with fireclay and overlain with brick clay in parts. In 1878 some 4,000 bricks were made and sold using this clay. The coal reserves were estimated at 4½ million tons from which it was said that 200 tons per day could be won if 70 men were employed! By 1881 the pit was employing more men, the work force comprising a colliery manager, a book keeper, 16 miners, one engineman, one blacksmith and one banks man [sic]. They were mainly housed, with their families, in the nearby terraced cottages, then known as the Longwitton Terrace Cottages (now Colliery East and Colliery West Cottages), though two miners lived in nearby Rothley.

The rail line to the colliery left the Rothbury branch just to the east of Longwitton, station. It made a sharp turn towards the south-east, crossing the Rothley Gill. The substantial embankment, on which the line was carried, forms the dam which has allowed the creation of Rothley Lakes, visible to the sides of the present day Scots Gap to Rothbury road (B6342). The line descended on a south-easterly route, passing through a shallow cutting and then emerging onto open moorland and crossing the Cleugh Burn near to its source. Eventually, near to Jock's Well, it swung round a curve to the left, to run parallel to the Longwitton road, until finally reaching the colliery. It is recorded that its completion occurred shortly after the completion of the shorter line to the limeworks. The layout of sidings at the colliery is not known, nor is it known whether the locomotive could be stabled here under cover. The cost of the works has also not been discovered.

The company locomotive referred to was *Longwitton*. This was an 0-4-0 saddle tank with two outside 8 in. cylinders. It was obtained new from Black, Hawthorn & Co. of Gateshead (Works No. 325/1875). Its work was divided between the colliery branch and the company's branch to the Greenleighton lime kilns (*see later volume*). It must therefore have had permission to pass through Longwitton station over the tracks of the North British Railway. Its fate, after the closure of the colliery and limeworks, is not known. Unfortunately no photographs of the locomotive have been discovered.

By 1883, under the ownership of the new consortium (*see page 121*), there were still eight hewers at work and some 27 tons of coal were won each day from the 'south end' of the colliery. The seam was said to be 2 ft 9 in. thick. In 1885 there were 16 hewers at work. Two horses and putters were employed and about 35 tons per day were being raised to the surface. Half of this coal was destined for the Greenleighton kilns. However, the pit closed during this year. An inventory was drawn up for the liquidators of the company which included the following entries:

123 tons of rail in the permanent way and sidings at the Colliery
2750 sleepers in the permanent way
1012 sleepers on the tramway
Grasshopper engine: 14″ cylinders, 3′ stroke
Wagons: 4 chaldron wagons; 3 box wagons
Tubs: 40 coal tubs (4½ hundredweight); one water tub frame
Loco engine: One locomotive engine by Black Hawthorn and Co of Gateshead; 8″ cylinders; firebox tubes recently renewed with one copper steam pipe and one set of old motion gear; Value: £375

Valuations included: 'Tubs: £61, Wagons: £15, 70lb Rails: £307/10/0d, Plates: £25, Sleepers: £51/11/3d, Tramway sleepers: £1/10/0d'.

After the closure of the colliery there was no further use for the line to the Rothbury branch and it was lifted except for a short stub at the station end. This could only be accessed by down trains on the branch.

The liquidators failed to find a buyer for the colliery and its buildings were demolished in 1886, though the *Newcastle Chronicle*, the *Journal*, the *Durham Chronicle* and the *Newcastle Daily Leader* all carried the following advert on 29th November, 1889:

Coal Royalty at Longwitton
To Let. Situate near Rothbury Branch of the North British Railway with Cottages. Apply to G.B. Forster Esq, North Jesmond, Newcastle upon Tyne.

Apparently several people enquired about leasing the colliery but no one took out a lease.

The electricity supply was removed in 1893 and by 1900 it was reported that there were no colliery 'erections' at the site, with the pit being inaccessible. Nine colliery cottages survived. The same source referred to seven 'old pits' surviving nearby, possibly old bell pits.

Today it is possible to follow the line of the colliery railway which is now a public bridleway between the colliery site and Longwitton station. Little remains at the colliery except for some building remains and mounds of spoil and the small pond formerly a reservoir for the pumping engine's water supply. The vicinity of the colliery is now part of an 'economic forestry scheme'. The embankment at the end of Rothley Lake is still impressive and can be seen, beyond the lake, from the Rothbury to Scots Gap road. Several of the former colliery cottages survive.

The site of the former Longwitton Pit can still be identified 100 metres to the north of the Rothley to Netherwitton Road. The location of the former shaft is surrounded by trees whilst the former colliery sidings were located in the low land to the left of the trees in the foreground.   *Author*

The spoil tip at Longwitton Colliery survives to the west of the former pit shaft. The railway sidings were located by the small conifer in the foreground of the picture.   *Author*

Acknowledgements

I would like to acknowledge with much gratitude the assistance provided by the following 'official' organizations, individuals and companies that have been very patient and generous in responding to requests for assistance with my research:

Northumberland Record Office at Woodhorn (formerly at Gosforth and Morpeth), Berwick-on-Tweed Record Office (Linda Bankier and Carole Pringle), Durham Record Office, Tyne & Wear Archives Service, Somerset Record Office, Powys County Archives, Northumberland County Libraries at Berwick-upon-Tweed, Morpeth and Alnwick, City of Dundee Library, British Library (Map Library and Newspaper Library, Colindale), the National Archives at Kew, the Parliamentary Archive, Dundee City Archive, Tweeddale Press Group (*Berwick Advertiser*), *Northumberland Gazette*, *The Times*, Lloyds Register of Shipping, Berwick-upon-Tweed Civic Society, Berwick-upon-Tweed Preservation Trust (John Smithson), the Ordnance Survey, Durham Mining Museum, Industrial Railway Society (Dave Holroyde), Industrial Locomotive Society (Russell Wear and Allan C. Baker), the Historical Model Railway Society (Peter Swift), North of England Open Air Museum at Beamish, National Railway Museum Library, Companies House, Narrow Gauge Railway Society (Clive Walters), the Ruston Archive (Ray Hooley), Devon Railway Centre, Fife Family History Society, Scottish Stone Liaison Group, Smiths Gore (James Boulton), Plateway Press, Forestry Commission (Kielder District), Australian War Memorial Research Centre, National Railway Museum (C.P. Atkins), Department of Veterans Affairs in Canberra, Australia (Richard Reid), Royal Artillery Museum (Matthew Buck and Paul Evans), Berwick-upon-Tweed Museum, Berwick-upon-Tweed Corporation (Freemen) Trustees, Wooler Information Centre, Glendale Gateway Trust, Northumberland County Council Conservation Team, Alan Keef Ltd, Northumberland National Park Authority, Northumbrian Water, Newcastle Local Studies Centre, Defence Estates, Ministry of Defence (Chris Livsey), Public Monument and Sculpture Association, Directorate of History and Heritage of the Canadian Department of National Defence, National Library of Canada and National Archives of Canada, Northumbria Rail, Aln Valley Railway Society (Vera Mallon, Gavin Head, Ken Middlemist and William Stafford), Road Roller Association, the Geological Society of London, British Geological Survey, Building Research Establishment, the Lagan Group, TARMAC Ltd, Hanson UK (David Weeks), Stirling Stone Group, LH Group Services (Henry Noon), Howick Estates, Northumberland Estates, Wallington Estates, Joicey Estates, Lilburn Estates Farming Partnership, Chillingham Castle (Sir Humphrey Wakefield), George F. White (Land Agents), Bailiffgate Museum in Alnwick (Gemma Taylor), the Thorneycroft Register (Alan Sleight), Whitstable Museum (Craig Bowen), Railsearch Images (Thomas Carrick), The Irving Gallery, the Road Locomotive Society, the Royal Forestry Society, the National Trust (Harry Beamish), Leather Family Archives (Michael Greene), Belford Local History Society (Fiona Renner-Thompson), Taylor Wimpey, Bamburgh Golf Club (the late Gordon McKeag), Glasgow University Archive Services, Derbyshire Local Studies Library, and the Mitchell Library in Glasgow.

I have made use of the website of the Durham Mining Museum, the 'keystothepast' website of the Northumberland and Durham County Councils, and the 'Northumberland Communities' website of the Northumberland Archive Service. The website 'Access to Archives' (a2a) has been invaluable in enabling me to identify and locate a huge variety of documents. The internet, generally, has been a valuable research tool allowing me to access records, for example in Canada and Australia, which I would not otherwise have discovered. I have used census records available both on CD-ROM and on-line.

The records of the Industrial Railway Society, the Industrial Locomotive Society and the Narrow Gauge Railway Society have been invaluable in providing me with details of the various locomotives mentioned in the text. In return I have been pleased to pass on to them details which have not previously been in their records, or corrections arising out of my research. In particular I offer my grateful thanks to Dave Holroyde of the IRS and NGRS who kindly read through much of the manuscript, offered much helpful advice and corrected locomotive and other details.

In a recently published book on railways, an author apologized for not including the names of all of the '101 private individuals' who had provided assistance with his book. I would like to offer my grateful thanks to the 202 individuals (at least!) who have found the time to provide help during my eight years of research for this book. Your assistance, your letters, your emails and your telephone calls have been very much appreciated. Those who have offered photographs for the book will see their name appearing beneath those that have been used. If a photograph has not been used it may well have provided very useful information which I have incorporated into the book. If you have provided me with information, or directed me towards sources of information, I'm sure you will be pleased to recognise the relevant material in the text.

It is likely that there will be some errors or omissions. For these I accept full responsibility. I would be delighted to receive any photographs, corrections or additions which would make the descriptions of these minor railways more complete.

Every attempt has been made to identify the copyright owners of the illustrations used. However, some were obtained from unmarked photographic prints or old picture postcards purchased, for example, at postcard fairs. Often these have no means of identification and have thus been described as being from the 'author's collection'. My sincere apologies if your print has been used without permission.

Abbreviations for Locomotive Builders

AB	Andrew Barclay, Sons & Co. Ltd, Kilmarnock
CE	Clayton Equipment, formerly Clarke Chapman Ltd, Clayton Works, Derby
EE	English Electric Works, Preston
EEV	English Electric Works, Newton-le-Willows
HC	Hudswell, Clarke & Co. Ltd, Leeds
HE	Hunslet Engine Co. Ltd, Leeds
HL	R. & W. Hawthorn, Leslie & Co. Ltd, Newcastle-upon-Tyne
MW	Manning, Wardle & Co. Ltd, Leeds
NB	North British Locomotive Co. Ltd, Glasgow
P	Peckett & Sons Ltd, Bristol
RS	Robert Stephenson & Co. Ltd, Newcastle-upon-Tyne
RSH	Robert Stephenson & Hawthorns Ltd
RSHN	Robert Stephenson & Hawthorns, Newcastle-upon-Tyne (successors to Hawthorn, Leslie & Co. Ltd)
VF	Vulcan Foundry Ltd, Newton-le-Willows
WB	W.G. Bagnall Ltd, Stafford
WR	Wingrove & Rogers Ltd, Kirkby, Liverpool

Bibliography

The following books and journals, in whole or in part, contain further reading or photographs related to some of the minor railways and industries in Northern Northumberland; all of these have been consulted.

The North British Railway in Northumberland by G.W.M. Sewell: Merlin Books
Main Line Railways of Northumberland by C.R. Warn: Frank Graham
Waggonways and Early Railways of Northumberland by C.R. Warn: Frank Graham
Rural Branch Lines of Northumberland by C.R. Warn: Frank Graham
Railways of the Northumberland Coalfield by C.R. Warn: Frank Graham
Industrial Railways in Northumberland and County Durham in the Days of Steam by Malcolm Castledine: Book Law Publications
A Regional History of the Railways of Great Britain: Volume IV The North East by Ken Hoole: David & Charles
Railway Stations of the North East by Ken Hoole: David & Charles
Forgotten Railways, North East England by Ken Hoole: David & Charles
Lindisfarne's Limestone Past by Roger C. Jermy: Northumberland Libraries
Lindisfarne Holy Island by Deidre O'Sullivan and Robert Young: English Heritage
Railways in Northumberland by Alan Young: Martin Bairstow Publishing
The Alnwick to Cornhill Railway 1887 to 1953 by Mary H. Brown: The Aln and Breamish Local History Society
The Alnwick and Cornhill Railway by John Addyman and John Mallon: North Eastern Railway Association
Industrial Locomotives of Northumberland: compiled by L.G. Charlton and Colin E. Mountford: Industrial Railway Society (a new edition, compiled and edited by Dave Holroyde, is in preparation)
Lost Railways of Northumberland by Robert Kinghorn: Countryside Books
Industrial Archaeology of North-East England (Volumes 1 & 2) by Frank Atkinson: David & Charles
Dam Builders' Railways from Durham's Dales to the Border by H.D. Bowtell: Plateway Press
The North Sunderland Railway by A. Wright: Oakwood Press
The Rothbury Branch by S.C. Jenkins: Oakwood Press
The Amble Branch by Bartle Rippon: Kestrel Railway Books
The Alnwick Branch by Bartle Rippon: Kestrel Railway Books
Border Country Branch Line Album by Neil Caplan: Ian Allan
Middleton, The Leathers and the Colonel's Railway by Tony Lee: Belford Local History Society
Memories of the LNER in Rural Northumberland by Allan Stobbs: published by the author
The Collieries of Northumberland Vol. 1 by James Tuck: Trade Union Printing Services
Longframlington: A look at the village through photos and stories by John West: published by the author
Wooler to Hexham and Return by Ken Veitch: The John Sinclair Railway Museum, Killingworth
Views of Wooler and Glendale by Derek Fairnington and Roger Mikel: MacLean Press, Wooler
Reflections, The Breamish Valley and Ingram by Sarah Wilson: Northern Heritage
We Can Mind The Time; Memories of Craster People: Ed. Colin Biott: Craster Community Development Trust
A History of Northumberland and Newcastle Upon Tyne by Leslie W. Hepple: Phillimore & Co.
Colliery Engineering: November 1930 Edition
Railway Bylines: various editions: Irwell Press

Various newspapers have been consulted including copies of the *Berwick Advertiser*, the *Northumberland Gazette* and the *Cumberland News*, also trade journals including the *Stone Trade Journal, Contract Journal* and *Machinery Market*.

Bound volumes of the *Berwick Advertiser* are located in the offices of the company which still produces this newspaper in Berwick, though it is probably easier to conduct inspections at Berwick Public Library or at Berwick Record Office where most editions of this newspaper (and others covering the local area) are available on microfilm. It is advisable to book ahead to reserve a microfilm reader at both places.

Bound volumes of the *Northumberland Gazette* (and other early local newspapers which covered the Alnwick area) are held at the Bailiffgate Museum in Alnwick although they are not currently available for inspection. A few bound volumes, free to view, are kept at Alnwick Public Library. Other editions have been microfilmed and are available for inspection at the same library.

Microfilm copies of Berwick, Alnwick, Carlisle, Gateshead and Newcastle newspapers, also other journals, can be viewed at the Newspaper Library in Colindale, London, though it is essential to make reservations in advance.

The many original documents consulted can be found at various locations, including the Berwick-on-Tweed Record Office, the Northumberland Record Office at Woodhorn (formerly at Gosforth and Morpeth), the Durham University Archive, the National Archives at Kew, and in other public and private collections (see 'Acknowledgements'). Many of the colliery records, formerly with the Northumberland Record Office, have been moved recently to the North of England Institute of Mining and Mechanical Engineers in Westgate Road, Newcastle-upon-Tyne.

The closure of the Shilbottle and Whittle collieries did not mean 'the end of the line' for 0-6-0 saddle tank RSH 7763 which was preserved in working order at the Tanfield Railway in County Durham. The locomotive is pictured here, in August 1986, outside the locomotive shed at Marley Hill, before working a train to Sunniside.   *Author*